Target Band 7

IELTS Academic Module - How to Maximize Your Score

Third Edition

Simone Braverman

www.IELTS-Blog.com

D1434525

Author Note

Correspondence concerning this book should be addressed to Simone Braverman
at simone@ielts-blog.com

Target Band 7
IELTS Academic Module - How to Maximize Your Score (Third Edition)
ISBN 978-0-9873009-6-6
© July 2015 by Simone Braverman

Limits of Liability/ Disclaimer of Warranty

From the author

I am very grateful for all the help and support I've received from all the members of my team, namely:

Vladimir Levitin - for great research
Roman Itskovich and Gregory Braverman - most talented Internet gurus
Nataly Dehter-Vaksman - for excellent legal advice
Eduard and Dina Somin - for superb ideas

Together there is no mountain we can't climb!

Acknowledgements

Thanks to the many authors, organizations and websites that have so kindly permitted us to use their material in our test, or allowed us to use the material under a creative commons license / public domain.

Endangered Sharks in Australia - http://www.environment.gov.au, http://www.supportoursharks.com
Flexible Working in our Workplace - http://www.acas.org/
A Threatened Breed (Polar Bears) http://www.wwf.org.uk/
Biodegradable Plastic - http://www.copyrightfreecontent.com, http://www.ncbi.nlm.nih.gov, http://green-plastics.net - Greg Stevens at Green Plastics
The Australian Pearl Industry - http://www.australia.gov.au
Blood Type Dieting - http://www.weightlossresources.co.uk, http://www.ncbi.nlm.nih.gov
Academic Writing - http://www.publications.parliament.uk, http://commons.wikimedia.org/wiki/File:Current_typical_floor_plan,_2013.jpg

Table of Contents

What this book is about

This guide is here to teach you the IELTS test, not the English language. Why?
Even if English is your first language, you can forget about getting a good score in IELTS, unless you are prepared for it. Three main problems will get in your way: *time, tricks and logical traps*.

When it comes to IELTS, **time is your worst enemy**. You need to do things fast. Of course you would get all the answers right if you had the time. But the reality is that there are a lot of questions to be answered, a lot of writing to be done, and very little time to do it.

This guide teaches you **HOW TO**:
- Listen, hear the right answers and write them down FAST
- Scan through the text and deal with all kinds of questions FAST
- Get your essay written FAST
- Build a speech in your head on any topic FAST
- Know and avoid the traps when you see them

This book might not make your English perfect, but it will certainly help you to get in shape and get your target Band Score!

Attitude tips

In my opinion (which was validated by the IELTS scores of the people I trained) you don't need more than 4 weeks of daily training. Set aside 3 hours that you devote to practice for IELTS - and it will get you the desired result.

I believe that if you can read and understand this e-book, your English is good enough. Just stick to the guidelines of this book and they will help you get the best IELTS score you can with your current level of English. You can even give yourself a *day off* once a week, and still be able to ace the IELTS!

To receive free IELTS advice and updates to your email go to http://www.ielts-blog.com and subscribe. You will be pleasantly surprised by the amount of useful information and friendly support you will receive.

How to use this book

The way this manual has been put together makes it possible for you to read the main chapters (Listening, Reading, Writing or Speaking tips) in **any** order you like - each is completely independent of the other. You don't have to follow the order in which the book is written.

If you don't have much time, I suggest reading this book and doing only the exercises that are included in it, no extra work. This is not the ideal way though. In case you do have the time, I highly recommend that you read and pay attention to all the tips in this manual and then try to use them when you practice real IELTS tests. There are links to IELTS materials at the end of every main chapter and a detailed study plan at the end of the book.

At the end of the book there are Pocket tips - short summaries of the most important hints in each of the chapters - Listening, Reading, Writing or Speaking. Every time you practice, read them before you start a test - they will refresh your memory and focus you on what's really important. Enjoy!

The IELTS Routine

The IELTS test consists of four parts: **Listening, Reading, Writing** and **Speaking.**

Listening takes about 40 minutes - 30 minutes to listen to a recording and to answer questions on what you hear, and 10 minutes to transfer your answers to the Answer Sheet.

Reading takes 1 hour and your task is to read passages of text and to answer questions according to what you have read. There are also other types of assignment which I will cover later on.

Writing also takes 1 hour and is divided into 2 sub-parts: 20 minutes to write a report and 40 minutes to write an essay.

Speaking takes up to 15 minutes and consists of 3 parts: a Personal Interview, a Short Speech and a Discussion.

All the parts continue one after another, and only before the Speaking do you get a little break. In some cases the Speaking section is held on a different day.

The Listening test at a glance

The Listening test consists of 4 sections. There are 40 questions in total. You need to answer all the questions as you listen to the recording. The recording is not paused at any time and you hear it only once. The questions get more difficult as you progress through the test.

Are you scared yet? Don't be! There is a technique to get you through it. Just make sure that your answers are readable and easy to understand when you copy them to the Answer Sheet. You may write in **pencil only**.

The Reading test at a glance

The Reading test consists of 3 text passages and has 40 questions in total. Your job is to read the passages and either answer questions, label diagrams, complete sentences or fill gaps. For every type of task there are instructions and an example. Passages are taken from books, newspapers, magazines and the topics are very diverse, from scuba diving to space exploration. Passages progress in difficulty, with the first being the easiest and the third the hardest.

The good news is that you don't really have to read the whole passage, thanks to techniques that I will refer to later. The not so good news is that there is no additional time to copy your answers to the Answer Sheet and you need to squeeze it into the 60 minutes that you have. Please, don't forget to do this - I witnessed someone who did forget, and it was not a pretty sight. The poor guy was crying, he received a score of '0' for the **whole** Reading test. Here too you may write in **pencil only**, no pens are allowed.

The Writing test at a glance

The Writing test has 2 sub-tasks. The first one is to write a **report** based on a graph, a diagram or a table you receive, using about 150 words. The second task is to write an **essay** on a given topic, present and justify an opinion or give a solution to a problem, using no fewer than 250 words.

Nothing to worry about here! Once you start using a certain structure which I'll explain later on for the report and the essay, in addition to your imagination, it is a piece of cake. This task requires a bit of training, but after you have written a few essays and reports you will be well-prepared for the test and you will feel **confident**.

The Speaking test at a glance

This is the fun part of the test, for many reasons. You get to rest before it. You are a little tired from the previous 3 parts and therefore more relaxed. The examiners are trained to smile no matter what, so you feel as if you are speaking to your best friend.

The first sub-part of the Speaking test is an interview, which means that the examiner asks you questions about yourself, your work, studies, parents, brothers/sisters, pets, etc. This is an easy task to prepare for.

In the second sub-part of the Speaking test you receive a card with 3-4 questions. After one minute, during which you have to think about something to say, you should give a short speech for one to two minutes, which answers those questions. At the end the examiner might ask you a couple of additional questions.

In the third sub-part of the test you have a discussion with the examiner. The topic is somehow related to the one from section two, but it is about more abstract ideas. You have to express and justify your opinions.

The examiner will record your session. Don't worry about it; the recording is to test the examiner and not you.

Tips for the Listening Test

In general

The Listening Test is probably the one people get most scared of. To help yourself overcome that fear, start watching TV programs in English. These are better than radio or audio books, because you also see images that help you understand the words you hear.

Listening - a skill, not a gift!

From my experience, in many cases listening is the least developed skill. So if you feel especially weak in that area, pay attention to the following tips, as they will help you improve your Listening ability. Remember - nobody is born with it, it's just a skill and you learn it. If you think your listening needs no improvements - skip the "Teach yourself the words" part, move forward to the tips which follow that part.

Teach yourself the words

The only way to improve your Listening ability is to train your ears to separate and understand the words you hear in the flow of a sentence. Often what you hear is a "Blablablablabla", which you can't break into words, and for that reason it makes no sense to you. When training, make a recording of the news, a lecture, a television program, a movie or an actual IELTS Listening test and work with it. I suggest using an MP3 player. You can easily record English from the radio or any other source onto it. It is also easy to repeat (re-play) sentences you didn't understand. An MP3 player is small and light, so you can use it in any spare moment that you have - riding on a bus or on a tram, walking the dog, taking a walk, etc.

First, listen, remember what you heard and stop the recording after each phrase. Even if you didn't understand the phrase, play it in your head a couple of times, like a broken record - "Tonight we have a special guest", "Tonight we have a special guest", "Tonight we have a special guest". Then say it out loud. If you understood that phrase at first, this exercise will improve your pronunciation. If you didn't understand the phrase the first time, this repetition will give you more time to hear it better, break it into words and make sense out of them. If it is still difficult, you can always rewind and hear the phrase again.

There is a big difference between **seeing** a word printed on paper while reading, and **hearing** it. If you saw a word, it doesn't mean you will recognize it when you hear it.
This is why you must hear every word you have seen at least once.

Instructions will keep you safe

Every task in the IELTS Listening test has its instructions. It may sound stupid, but you really need to read them carefully. Why? Because they will tell you exactly what to do with the information: how many words you can use to answer questions, whether or not there is a table you must fill in, whether there is a list to choose words from, how many items you must name, etc. Remember, too, that if the answer must be in 3 words - write EXACTLY 3 WORDS, because writing four or two words will get you 0 score.

To make my point crystal clear, let's take the following scenario as an example:
The speaker on a recording says:
 "Well, if you are dieting, try to avoid fruits with lots of fructose like watermelon, mango, peaches or grapes."

The question in the booklet is:
"Name 2 fruits a person on a diet should not eat".

The answer may be "watermelon, mango" or "mango, peaches" or any combination of **two** items, but **never three or four**!!! Anyone who writes "watermelon, mango, peaches, grapes", just to be on the safe side, receives a score of zero for that question.

Note: when counting words - "a", "the" or a number (e.g. 159) is considered a word.

When instructions say "a maximum of 3 words" or "no more than 3 words" - you can write one, two or three words, but **never** more than three.

Divide and conquer!

The recording divides questions into **groups,** so for every grouping you are instructed to answer 4-5 questions. There are 20-30 seconds of silence before each group.

The first thing you should do when the recording starts playing, is understand which group of questions you need to answer.

For example, the recording says: "Look at questions one to four". It means that you have about 20 seconds to look at those questions. Go over the questions, read them and underline keywords. Keywords are the words that contain the main idea of the question. They will help you guess what you will hear - numbers, opening hours, names, locations, etc.

Draw a line under the fourth question, so you won't look further before it's time to do so.

Next you will hear a piece of spoken language and answer the questions one to four **as you listen.** It means that you should be able to write one answer and listen to another.

After that, the recording will say the numbers of the questions in the next group. Repeat the same process, including drawing the line. This dividing technique is very efficient because every time you concentrate on a **limited** number of questions, it makes you more focused and in control.

Distractions

Don't get confused by all the different voices you are going to hear. The recording uses several different voices - of younger and older people, men and women. You may also hear different accents - Australian, British, American, Japanese, etc. The background noises also vary. They can be from an airport, a coffee-shop, a street, a university lecture hall, you name it. Be ready for it and don't let it distract you - because that is exactly what they want. Ignore the noises and listen for the answers.

Listen for specifics

When you are listening, look for descriptions and details, such as dates, places, telephone numbers, opening hours, years (1995), transportation (car, bike, train), etc.
If you hear them, but don't know where to place them yet - write them in the margins of the Listening booklet. Later you will have some time to check your answers. Going over the questions that you couldn't answer during the Listening passage, you might see if what you've written in the margins fits.

Answer as you listen

The reason you have to "answer as you listen" is that you immediately forget the sentences after you have heard them - because of stress, foreign language, constant flow of information, etc. After hearing the third sentence you won't be able to repeat the first. It means that when any part of the Listening is over you won't be able to remember any of the answers. So write them as you hear them, leave nothing for later.

Keep moving forward

A worst case scenario is you "losing the sequence of answers" - so you miss one answer and then you miss another one and so on. To prevent this from happening, always look one or two questions ahead. It sounds confusing, but after a little practice it becomes very natural and helps a lot. Even if you have missed the answer to a question - **admit it** and move to the next one, otherwise you will lose it too.

Know your clues

The answer is usually pronounced **louder and clearer**, so it is easier to hear and understand. If you can't hear something clearly (because the speaker swallows words or whispers), then probably the answer is not there. With some practice you will be able to tell the difference.

A good clue to an answer is when you hear a repetition of a word, a word being **spelled** out (G A R F U N K E L) or a number **dictated**.

Spelling tasks

As simple as it sounds, the spelling task is not so easy. You should practice a little to be prepared for it. Just ask someone to spell the names of cities from the following list for you. If you study alone, you could record yourself spelling those names and numbers, and then play it. The same goes for the list of telephone numbers I've included here. It is good practice and will only add to your confidence. Note: in numbers, '00' is sometimes read as "double o" instead of "zero-zero".

Cities	Numbers
Antananarivo	423-5207-0074
Brazzaville	628-2087-2311
Conakry	5167-832-0155
Gaborone	8746-221-0302
Johannesburg	5337-298-0132
Kinshasa	5900-231-7621
Libreville	4348-663-980
Lilongwe	11-267-55410
Mogadishu	101-9020-7624
Ouagadougou	413-2567-9011

Typical Listening tasks

Do you remember my promise - no surprises in IELTS? The following table shows you every type of task you may see in the Listening test booklet. Different task types come with different instructions, so if you see and remember them now, it will save you time later.

Of course, you won't get every type I show here in your test and the table looks a bit boring.
Anyway, my advice is to get to know them **now**.
Don't let them catch you off-guard!

Task Type	What you should do	Instructions in the booklet
Selecting pictures	From 3-4 pictures choose a picture that best describes what you hear.	Circle the appropriate letter.
Multiple choice questions	There is a question and a number of answers (three, four or five), your job is to pick the right one (sometimes more than just one).	Circle the appropriate letter /Circle the correct answer.
Short-answer questions	Answer in 1, 2 or 3 words, as the instructions say.	Complete the notes/table. Use NO MORE THAN 3 WORDS for each answer.
Sentence completion	Complete a sentence according to what you hear.	Complete the notes/table. Use NO MORE THAN 3 WORDS for each answer.
Form completion	A form is given and you need to fill in blank fields.	Complete the form. Write NO MORE THAN 3 WORDS for each answer.
Chart/Table completion	A table with some blank cells is given; your job is to fill them according to the passage you hear.	Complete the notes/table. Use NO MORE THAN 3 WORDS for each answer.
Gap-fill	There are several sentences with missing words. You should pick the correct word and write it in the gap. Choose from the list (if there is one), or from what you have heard.	Complete the notes below by writing NO MORE THAN 3 WORDS in the spaces provided.
Diagram labeling	Write a description of 1, 2 or 3 words for different parts of a drawing according to what you hear.	Complete/label the diagram by writing NO MORE THAN 3 WORDS in the boxes/spaces provided.

Note: in some cases instructions in the booklet will indicate a different word limit for your answer.

For example: "Use NO MORE THAN 2 WORDS AND/OR A NUMBER for each answer".

Eliminate wrong answers

When you deal with multiple-choice questions, elimination is a good strategy.
Usually only one answer is correct, unless the instructions say something else.

This task can be done using the True/False/Not Given technique. In multiple choice questions consider each option and ask yourself whether it is true, false or not given according to the passage. Of course the one option that is true is the correct answer! Any other answer is obviously incorrect.

Keep in mind that there are cases when all the choices are correct or none of them is correct. Read the instruction carefully and you will know what to do in such cases.

Gap-fill strategy

Look at the words around the gap to understand what's missing, a noun (like boy, toy, truck), an adjective (little, pretty, shiny) or a verb (stands, looks, moves).

For instance, if you see a **Noun** before the blank ("The boy is___"), it means that it's an **Adjective** ("The boy is **small**") or it's a **Verb** ("The boy is **smiling**") that is missing.

Once you have picked a word, write it above the gap and then read the whole sentence to be sure that it makes sense.

Check the grammar

If the answer you give is grammatically incorrect - it cannot be the right one. Checking the grammar of your answers will give you an idea whether your answer is correct or not, especially in tasks like:
- Gap-fill
- Sentence completion

Use your time wisely

During the test, you have a little time between Listening sections. Use it to check and complete your answers.

"Chameleon" questions

They might use different words with the same meaning to confuse you. It could be expressions or synonyms.

For example, the recording might say "All the candidates **have to** fill an application form" and the question says "The candidates **must** fill an application" - is it True, False or Not Given? The correct answer is True because **"have to"** means **"must"**.

Watch out for traps

Trap Number One - unexpected turn

You might hear a speaker starting to say one thing and then, suddenly, continuing to something completely different. This is a trap, so make sure you don't fall for it. The rule here is "The last word counts". For example, if the speaker says "I want to visit that gallery on Monday. No, wait, I've just remembered that it is closed on Monday, so I will go on Wednesday.", and the question is "When...?" - the correct answer here is Wednesday, and Monday is a trap.

Trap Number Two - generalizations

You might hear a speaker first give a list of things and then say them **all in one word**. For example: "Well, I like to swim, hike, and camp - to be involved in outdoor activities." If the question is "What kind of activities…" the correct answer is "outdoor" and not "swimming", "hiking" or "camping".

Trap Number Three - explicit answer choices

Explicit answer choices can be (and mostly will be) traps. The following example demonstrates what I mean:
The recording says: "This course is a must for all the first year students, excluding foreign students".
The Question is "**All** the first year students have to take this course",
The Answer should be **F**(alse), because there is an exception - foreign students.
All the explicit answers that mean "no exceptions" are a bit suspicious and call for more attention.

Copy answers smartly

After 30 minutes or so of the Listening test, there are 10 additional minutes. During the test you have written all of the answers in the Listening test booklet. These 10 minutes are given you to copy your answers onto the Answer Sheet, and you should use them **smartly**.

The Answer Sheet has 2 sides, one for the Reading test and one for the Listening test, so make sure you are writing on the Listening side. I include here an example of an Answer Sheet so you can get familiar with it and use it for practicing. First, copy all the answers from the booklet onto the Answer Sheet, and pay attention to the following guidelines (as simple as they sound - they are BIG time savers):

- For multiple-choice questions and picture selection questions - just copy the letter of the correct answer, don't circle it.
- For sentence completion - just copy your answer, not the whole sentence.
- For True/False/Not Given questions - just copy T, F or NG, whatever your choice is.
- For gap-fills - just copy the word you have chosen for the gap.
- For answers written in short (like prof. advice) - write the full version (professional advice).
- Check that all the answers are clear and understandable.

Now, if you missed some questions - it is a good time to guess.

The Answer Sheet looks like this:

1		21	
2		22	
3		23	
4		24	
5		25	
6		26	
7		27	
8		28	
9		29	
10		30	
11		31	
12		32	
13		33	
14		34	
15		35	
16		36	
17		37	
18		38	
19		39	
20		40	

For those of you who wonder why all the answers have to consist of a **maximum of 3 words** - here is the answer: there is not enough space on the Answer Sheet for anything longer than that!

Practice, practice, practice!

I strongly recommend that you use all the tips while practicing. In order to practice you are going to need samples of the Listening test, which can be found on the following internet sites (good quality, free of charge):

http://ielts-blog.com/online-practice/ - choose course type (General/Academic), then click on a big square button that says "FREE"
http://www.ieltsgym.com/?id=FreeEnglishlessons - online exercises with answers
http://www.esl-lab.com/- for this one you will need a Real Audio Player
http://www.ieltsontrack.com/mini_test.php?module=1 - a test with a transcript

Play the Listening samples and start using the tips while searching for answers. This is the only way to really understand how these tips work. You may have to play the same Listening file more than once, to practice different techniques.

Tips for the Reading Test

Test structure

Academic Reading in most cases consists of 3 large passages taken from newspapers or magazines. The first passage usually is the easiest and the last one is the most difficult.

As in the Listening test, questions in the Reading test are arranged in groups. Instructions will tell you which group of questions belongs to which paragraph or portion of text. You may see the questions **before** or **after** the passage they belong to.

Manage your own time

As I said before, time is your greatest enemy. In the Listening test it was managed for you, but the Reading test is a different story. You need to manage it very carefully yourself and this is where the **"15-20-25" rule** comes in.

When you receive the Reading booklet, first of all, count how many passages there are. Typically there are 3 passages in the booklet. You could divide the hour into 3 equal parts and spend 20 minutes on each passage, but this is not the smartest way. The **smartest** way is to spend 15 minutes on the first passage, 20 minutes on the second and 25 on the last one. Why? Because they progress in level of difficulty!

Write down the time when you should start and when you should finish working on each passage and stick to it. In each passage set aside 2 minutes to copy your answers to the Answer Sheet. For example, in the first paragraph you should use 13 minutes to actually answer the questions (writing the answers on the booklet pages) and 2 to copy your answers to the Answer Sheet.

If you didn't finish a passage in time, move to the next one anyway. And whatever you do, please do not forget about the Answer Sheet (remember the guy with the ZERO score?)

If you have some time left by the end of the Reading test, make sure that you didn't forget to answer any question. Check and double check your answers. It can give you a few "easy" points if you find mistakes before the examiner does.

Don't read - scan!

It sounds absurd that you don't need to read in a Reading test, right?
Anyway, it's true. The biggest mistake you could make is to start the test by reading the whole passage.

The best thing is to scan the text quickly. Don't try to understand every word! Just go over it and get the idea of what each paragraph is about. Usually you don't need to read the whole paragraph - the first couple of sentences are enough.

Make a map

The text before you resembles a strange, new territory. It is so easy to get lost inside all these words! What you need is a map that will help you to orientate. Every paragraph in the passage has its own main idea, which is different from all the other paragraphs. Write in the margins near the paragraph what its topic is, and its main idea. If writing takes too much time, underline the words in the paragraph that explain its main idea. Congratulations! You have just created a map that will later guide you through the search for answers.

Learn the rules

First, read the instructions and the example. They show you exactly what your answer should look like - is it a number or a name, how many words must you write, etc. The following points are important because they may affect your score.

1.   Style

When filling in the answers, **copy the example's style**. To demonstrate, look at the following table:

	USA	Canada	Sweden
Divorce rate	*Example 1*: **55%**		
Marriage	*Example 2*: **first**		

Example 1

If the example says "55%", give your answer in this exact form, a number and %. Any other form or style (like "55" or "55 percent" or "fifty five percent") may harm your score!

Example 2

If the example says "first", answering in any other form or style (like "1st", "1" or "first marriage") may harm your score.

2.   Word Limit

Usually if there is a word limit for an answer, it is no more than 3 words. Prepositions (in, of, to, at, etc), articles (a, an, the) and numbers (5, 12, etc) are considered words. The reason behind this 3 word limit is the limited space on the Answer Sheet.

3.   One question - One answer

Don't give more than one answer to one question, even if you see more than one option. It will result in a ZERO score. For example, if you see names of 3 countries that qualify as an answer and the question asks to name just one - don't even think of giving 2 or 3 names, the only correct answer is to name exactly one. Only if they ask for two names should you name two, etc.

Types of tasks

The kinds of task you may have to deal with are in the table below. Different task types come with different instructions. It is important for you to see them all **now**, so nothing will surprise you during your IELTS test. Understanding in advance what you need to do in every type of task gives you a huge advantage. This way during the test you will only read the instructions to **confirm** what you already know.

Task Type	What you should do	Instructions in the booklet
Matching	There is a list of headings, your job is to choose the most suitable heading for every paragraph of the text.	Choose the most suitable heading for each paragraph from the list of headings below.
Multiple choice questions	There is a question and a number of answers (three, four or five), your job is to pick the right one (sometimes more than just one).	Choose the appropriate letter.
Short-answer questions	Answer in 1, 2 or 3 words, as the instructions say.	Using NO MORE THAN THREE WORDS answer the following questions.
Sentence completion	Complete a sentence according to what you read.	Complete the sentences below with words taken from the reading passage. Use NO MORE THAN THREE WORDS for each answer.
Chart/Table completion	A table with some blank cells is given; your job is to fill them according to the passage you read.	Complete the table/chart below using information from the Reading Passage. Use NO MORE THAN THREE WORDS for each answer.
True/False/Not Given questions	There is a statement, which can be True, False or Not Given in the passage; you need to decide according to what you read.	Read the passage and look at the statements below. Write TRUE if the statement is true, FALSE if the statement is false and Not Given if the information is not given in the passage.
Yes/No/Not Given questions	There are statements which can agree with the claims of the writer, contradict them or be unrelated to the writer's claims; you need to decide according to what you read.	Complete the summary below (choose your answers from the box at the bottom of the page).

Task Type	What you should do	Instructions in the booklet
Gap-fill	There are several sentences with missing words, you should pick the correct word and put it in the gap. Choose from the list (if there is one), or from the text.	Complete the summary below (Choose your answers from the box at the bottom of the page).
Diagram labeling	Write a description of 1, 2 or 3 words for different parts of a drawing according to what you read.	Label the diagram below. Use NO MORE THAN THREE WORDS from the passage for each answer.

Go fishing!

Now it is time to start "fishing" for answers. Read the questions one-by-one, for every question see what its theme is. Then find it (or something close to it) on your map - that is the paragraph to search for the answer.

Choose your battles

If any question takes you too much time - give up, move to the next one. Don't forget to mark it with some sign (like "?"), so you can identify it and come back to it later. There are a lot of questions and you might miss the easy ones if the hard ones take all of your time. Another reason to leave hard questions until later is that after you do all the easy ones, you know more about the text, so then solving the tricky questions might become easier.

Use the passage layout

Every text and every paragraph in it has a certain structure, meaning it is written according to some rules.

Usually the first paragraph contains the main idea of the passage and the author's opinion. The last paragraph often summarizes the main points of the passage.

Every paragraph has a structure that is similar to the structure of a whole text. It has an introduction, a body and a conclusion. The main idea can usually be found in the introduction. It means that if you want to understand quickly what a paragraph is about, it is enough to read only its introduction.

Find the keywords

Keywords are the main words in the question; they contain the most important information. For instance, in a question like "Employers are likely to employ graduates, who…" there are 3 keywords: **employers**, **employ** and **graduates**.

Identify keywords in each question and look for them in the text - the answer will be near. Don't stop after finding just one, continue to scan through the text - there might be more.

Strategy for the Matching task

First, read the instructions and the example. If the instructions say that a heading **cannot** be used more than once - cross the heading used in the example out of the list. This way you won't try to use it again by mistake (and believe me, it's a very common mistake!).

Second, return to the map you have prepared. Go over the text and look at your map to see what it says about the idea in the first paragraph. Go to the list of headings and choose the heading that has the meaning that is most similar to the idea on your map, write its number in the margins of the first paragraph. Now continue and do the same for the second paragraph, and so on.

Sometimes you will see that paragraph X *mentions* the same fact as the heading Y, *but only as additional information (not the main idea)*. It is a **trap** to make you choose heading Y for that paragraph X. It may sound confusing, but this **example** explains everything:

Paragraph X:
The end result says that 61.6% of the Dutch people vote tegen (against) the European Constitution, while 38.4% voted voor (for) the Constitution. Turnout was unexpectedly high, at 62.8%, more than the last three elections. The 'no' vote follows a similar vote in France last week that led to the resignation of the prime minister Jean-Pierre Raffarin.

Heading Y: Prime minister of France resigns

Explanation:
Although the resignation of the prime minister of France is mentioned in paragraph X, *it is not its topic*. The topic is the Dutch people voting for/against the constitution, which means that heading Y is not suitable for paragraph X.

If some paragraphs are hard to match - leave them alone, keep moving forward. Come back to them later.

When you have finished matching - check your answers carefully, because they can influence each other. Don't forget to copy the answers to the Answer Sheet.

Strategy for the True/False/Not Given task

To simplify it for you, if the statement **clearly** appears in text - it is True. If the text clearly says the **opposite** of the statement in the question - it is False, if you didn't find the statement to be either TRUE or FALSE - it is Not Given.

Every passage is divided into paragraphs and each paragraph usually contains an **answer to one question**. It means that if you have found an answer to question 1 in paragraph A, then the answer to question 2 will probably be in paragraph B. In many cases, when you don't see that the paragraph is confirming that the statement is either True or False, the answer is Not Given.

The best advice here is not to over think. Otherwise you might start building logical sequences that lead you in the wrong direction.

Strategy for the Multiple-choice task

Here too the True/False/Not Given technique is a big help. The difference is that you need to use it on each option. For every possible answer you need to decide, if it is True, False or Not Given in the text. Finally, the answers you have marked as False or Not Given are incorrect, and the ones you marked as True are correct.

Remember: it is True only when the passage says exactly the **same** thing, it is False when the passage says exactly the **opposite** and it is Not Given in any other case.

Keep in mind that there are cases when all the choices are correct or none of them is correct. Read the instructions carefully and you will know what to do in such cases.

Strategy for the Gap fills

First of all try to understand what the main idea of the first sentence is. Then find it on your map - this should take you to the paragraph that "hides" the answer.

Now, when you know **where** to look, you need to know **what** to look for. Look at the text around the gap to understand what's missing - a noun (like boy, toy, truck), an adjective (little, pretty, shiny) or a verb (stands, looks, moves).

For example, what is missing here: "She _____ around and saw him in the corner"?

You have 4 choices: happy, man, looked, smiled. It is clear that you need a verb here, but which one, "looked" or "smiled"? Now it is time to start reading the text.
Find where the example answer is and start there. Remember to read only the first, the second and the last sentence. Of course, "looked" is the right word!

Sometimes there are words near a gap that will give you a clue about what kind of word is missing. For example, "The main physical activities in the summer camp are fishing, _____ and swimming. Naturally, you will look for words that end with "ing" to fill the gap - like "hiking".

There are 2 types of gap-fills: 1) There is a **list** of words for you to choose from
  2) There is **no list**, you need to choose words from the text

When you choose a word from the list and the instructions say that every word is to be used **once** only, write it above the gap and cross it out from the list. If there is more than one possible answer - write them all and then decide which one is better.

If they don't give you a list, try to pick a word from the text. It is better than "inventing" it, because it saves time and your chances of being right are higher. After you have decided on the word that goes into the gap, read the whole sentence again. It must make sense according to the text, and it must be grammatically correct.

When you move forward to the second gap, keep in mind that usually there are no more than 2 gaps per paragraph. It means that if you have found the answer to the first gap in paragraph 1, the answer to the second gap will be in paragraph 2 and so on.

Assumptions are the mother of all mess-ups!

Don't assume you know the answer, search for it in the passage. When answering the questions, you must stick to the facts as they are written in the paragraph. Forget all about your personal knowledge and experience! Relying on your own knowledge is the most natural thing for you, so sometimes they use it in IELTS to trick you into making a choice according to what you know or believe and not according to the passage.

Practice, practice, practice!

Reading the text in the way I described in this chapter must become a second nature to you. The only way to make it happen is to practice using my tips while doing the Reading test.

When practicing, finish the Reading test and then check your answers according to the Answer key. Pay attention to those you've got **wrong**, not those you've got right - understand why you didn't do them right and try to remember, so that mistake won't be repeated.

Practice with a clock and copy your answers onto the Answer Sheet. You may use the one from the chapter on the Listening test; it is similar to the Reading test Answer Sheet.

In order to practice, use only Academic module reading tests and never General Training reading. Generally, you need to buy texts to practice on, but I have managed to find a few sources of free tests and recommend them to you.

http://ielts-blog.com/online-practice/ - choose course type (General/Academic), then click on a big square button that says "FREE"
http://www.ieltsgym.com/?id=FreeEnglishlessons
http://www.examenglish.com/IELTS/IELTS_reading_2.htm
http://www.ieltsontrack.com/mini_test.php?module=2

Tips for the Writing test

As you may remember, the Writing test of the Academic Module has 2 tasks:

Writing Task 1 - to write a report.
Writing Task 2 - to write an essay.

Writing a report must not take you more than 20 minutes, so there will be 40 minutes left for the essay. Usually, not all of us are good at writing reports, not to mention essays, let alone in English! Well, SURPRISE - there is a technique to it, making writing so simple, a monkey could do it. So let's get down to business.

First, some general guidelines

You will receive two Answer Sheets to write on - one for Writing Task 1, meaning report, and one for Writing Task 2, meaning essay. Keep your writing neat, clean and nice-looking. Leave a blank line between paragraphs and don't write in the margins of the Answer Sheet. Don't make a mess even if you have made a mistake - just cross it out once.

If there are instructions that say that you need to write about a number of things (let's say A, B, C) - do it, write about every one of them. It is important for your score. You need to show the examiner that you have read and understood the instructions; otherwise he or she might think that you didn't.

One of the most typical mistakes is to copy task instructions. It is absolutely forbidden, wastes precious time and people lose points for it. You can use what is written in task instructions only if you rephrase it.

Task length is very important, so if you cannot reach the required word limit (150 for a report, 250 for an essay), try to get close to it. A good way to quickly count the number of words in your task is to count the number of words in one line and then multiply by the number of lines.
For example, 10 words in one line x 25 lines = 250 words in total.

These simple rules apply to both report and essay. Stick to them, and your work will leave a good impression on the examiner.

Tips for Writing Task 1 - Report

The task here is to describe a graph in a report. The report is intended for a university lecturer, so the language you use should be appropriate.

Types of graph for the report

There are several different figures you can see in the Writing Task 1:

- Single line graph
- Double line graph
- Bar graph (Single, Double or Triple bar graph)
- Pie chart
- Table
- Process diagram
- Plan / map (often showing changes from past to present, or from present to future)

It is also possible for you to get 2 figures from this list, for instance, a single line graph and a pie chart. In that case your report should include both of them.

The following figures illustrate all types of graph:

Single line graph

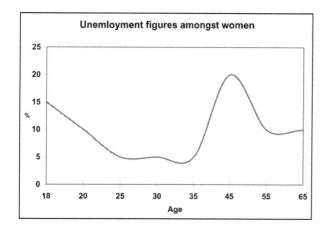

Double line graph

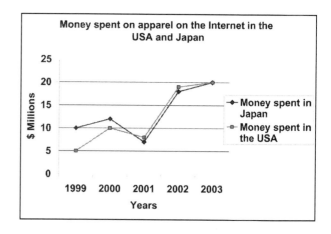

Single bar graph

Annual meat consumption in 7 countries (kg per person)

Double bar graph

Annual coffee and meat consumption in 7 countries

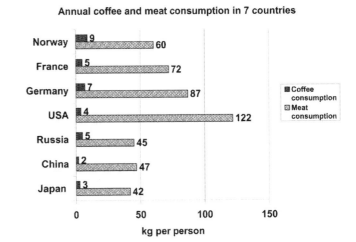

Pie chart

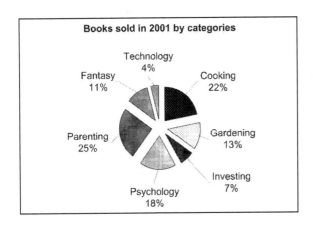

Table

Leisure time activities amongst women of various age groups

Leisure time activity	Age 20-25 %	Age 26-30 %	Age 31-40 %	Age 41-50 %
Watching TV	14	20	26	37
Reading	11	9	19	19
Gardening	1	3	5	7
Sports	17	26	2	1
Shopping	16	15	20	9
Cooking	2	5	10	16
Sewing	1	2	1	1
Entertaining	38	20	17	10

Process diagram

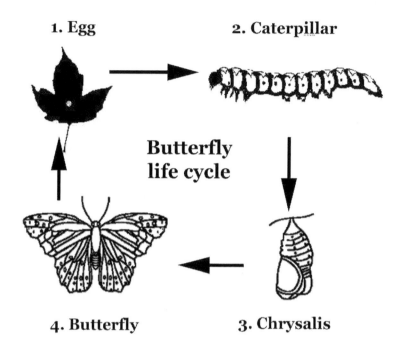

Plan / map

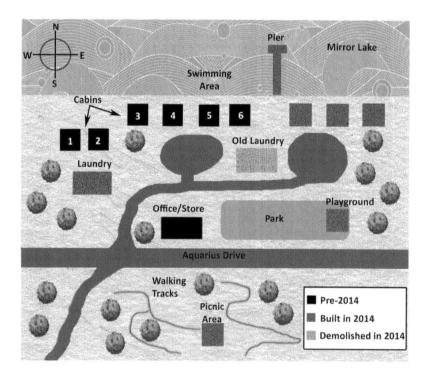

Universal rules

No matter what figure you are describing, you shouldn't break these rules:

- Your report must be of at least 150 words written in 20 minutes
- You shouldn't write your opinion or copy words from the graph - rephrase and use synonyms instead.
- Never use bullet points, write as if you were writing an essay.

What does a good report look like?

When your Academic Writing Task 1 is graded by IELTS examiners, they look for this structure:

1. Introduction (1 paragraph)

2. Body (may consist of 2-3 paragraphs)

3. Conclusion (1 paragraph)

The Introduction should describe the purpose of the report and say what overall trends you see. For example, if the trend in the graph is rising or falling, you should mention that. You need to remember that you are describing a graph to someone who doesn't see it, so your words must draw the picture. Write what the graph is about, its dates and location.

The Body should describe the most important trends, while all the information is summarized to avoid unnecessary details. For example, if there is a graph that has 2 peaks, you should mention them; say when those peaks appeared and what the peak values are.

Notice how many distinctive features the diagram has and divide the information into paragraphs, one paragraph for one feature (or a group of *similar* features). You should link the paragraphs by sentences that logically connect them to one another.

Important! You need to write about all the periods of time and all the subjects of the graph. If it shows several years (1992, 1993, 1994) - write about all of them, if it is about men and women - write about both. Remember, summarizing doesn't mean throwing away information. The secret here is to select what's important, organize it, compare and contrast.

The Conclusion should sum up the global trends shown and compare them if possible.

Your opinion shouldn't appear anywhere in the report. You also shouldn't include other information, that doesn't appear on the chart. This kind of writing can be (and probably will be) penalized!

"Time stamp" and grammar

The figure you need to write a report about always has a "time stamp" on it. This "time stamp" says to us that graph describes something that

1) Happened in the past
   OR
2) Continued in the past
   OR
3) Happens in the present
   OR
4) Will happen in the future

Example:

"Books sold in 2001 by categories" - happened in the past (1)

"The way people were spending money on clothes between 1999 and 2003" - continued in the past (2)

"Unemployment figures amongst women" - happens in the present, when there is **no time stamp we assume the present** (3)

"The map illustrates the proposed changes" – the changes will be made in the future (4)

You need to use correct tenses:

1) Happened in the past - use past simple.
2) Continued in the past - use past continuous.
3) Happens in the present - use present simple or present continuous.
4) Will happen in the future – use a future tense. Maps often require future passive (e.g. "will be built") or future simple (e.g. "will move from … to …"), other types of charts mostly require future simple.

Single line graph

How to start

"The graph **describes/shows/reveals** … (*what, who, when, where*). It can be clearly seen that … (*describe main trends here*).

Vocabulary

When describing such a graph, all you can say is that it either **rises (increases, climbs, goes up), falls (decreases, declines, drops, goes down), doesn't change (remains at the same level, maintains stability).** The highest point of a graph is a **peak** and the lowest is the **lowest point.** The speed of change also matters - you should say how **fast** (**rapidly**, **quickly**) or how **slowly** (**gradually**, **steadily**) it happened. And, of course, there is order to changes - a rise was **preceded by** a drop and **followed by** a decline.

How to describe trends

Numbers are boring, so you need to add a little "color" when describing them. By "color" I mean *comparison*. Don't just write "went from 100 in 1999 to 255 in 2001".
Write "increased by 155" or "had risen to 255".

Sample task

You should spend about 20 minutes on this task.

The graph on the right shows the unemployment figures amongst women of different age groups.

Write a report for a university lecturer describing the information shown.

You should write at least 150 words.

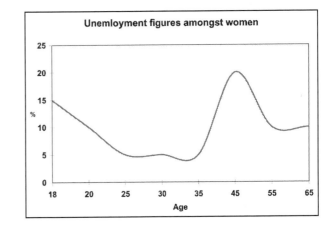

Sample answer:

The graph shows percentages of unemployed women at 8 ages. It can be clearly seen that the ages 18 and 45 have the highest unemployment rate.

According to the graph, among the ages 18, 20, 25, 30 and 35, the youngest women have the highest unemployment percentage (15%). 20 year-old women have much lower unemployment figures (about 10%), and percentages drop even lower (to 5 percent) for those aged 25 and 35. There is a slight increase for those aged 30, where the unemployment rate reaches 6 percent.

The peak value is recorded amongst 45 year-old women, and all the remaining ages have much lower figures: 8% at age 55 and 9% at age 65.

To sum up, the figures for most ages are relatively uniform and change from 5 to 9 %, with rare exceptions such as the ages 18 and 45.

Double line graph

How to start

"The graph **compares** … (*what, who, when, where*). It can be clearly seen that … (*describe main trends of 2 graphs here*).

Vocabulary

The same as for the single line graph description.

How to compare trends

In the body of the report start your first paragraph by describing the first graph.
In the next paragraph, if the 2 graphs are similar, write "*Similarly,*" and describe the other graph. If the 2 graphs are different, write "*In contrast,*" and describe the other graph.

You should also compare the peaks and troughs of the two graphs, see example below.

Sample task

You should spend about 20 minutes on this task.

The graph on the right shows the amounts spent on clothes on the Internet in the USA and Japan between 1999 and 2003.

Write a report for a university lecturer describing the information shown.

You should write at least 150 words.

Money spent on apparel on the Internet in the USA and Japan

Sample answer:

The graph compares amounts of money spent online on clothes in the USA and Japan starting from 1999 and until 2003. It is clear that although at first Japanese buyers were spending much more money than Americans did; as the years went by the spending habits of the 2 countries became almost identical.

In 1999 Japan was spending on clothes almost twice as much as the USA (10 versus 5 million dollars). In the following year the expenditure on clothes in both Japan and USA grew even further to 12 and 10 million dollars respectively.

The only year when expenses plunged in both countries was 2001, when the USA spent only 8 and Japan reached its lowest point at 7 million.

The two following years, 2002 and 2003 showed a rapid increase in sales of clothes in both countries. In 2002 the USA spent about 19 million dollars and Japan's numbers were very close (18 million). Online clothes sales became even more popular in 2003, pushing the figures higher to its peak of 20 million dollars in both Japan and the USA.

Bar graph

How to start

For a single bar graph: "The graph **describes/shows/reveals** … (*what, who, when, where*). It can be clearly seen that … (*describe main trends here*).

For multiple bars graphs: "The graph **compares** … (*what, who, when, where*). It can be clearly seen that … (*describe main trends here*).

Vocabulary

The same as for single line graph descriptions.

How to describe or compare trends

If the axis of the bar graph is a time scale - describe how the graph's subject changes in time. Otherwise compare the bars differently - more, less, most, least, etc, in order of appearance.

Sample task

You should spend about 20 minutes on this task.

The bar chart on the right shows figures of annual coffee and meat consumption.

Write a report for a university tutor describing the information shown.

You should write at least 150 words.

Annual coffee and meat consumption in 7 countries

Sample answer:

The bar chart compares the amounts of coffee and meat consumed every year in Norway, France, Germany, the USA, Russia, China and Japan.

It can be clearly seen that the lowest rates of coffee consumption are recorded in China and Japan (2 and 3 kg per person respectively). The next three countries have higher rates, consumption of coffee in the USA totals 4 kg per person, while France and Russia have equal consumption rates of 5 kg per person. The highest numbers belong to Germany and Norway, at 7 and 9 kg per person respectively.

Meat consumption numbers are much higher in all countries; the highest numbers are recorded in the USA (122 kg per person) and the lowest in Japan. Meat consumption in Russia (45) and China (47) is similar to that of Japan (42). Three other countries have much higher numbers, starting with Norway (60) and progressing through France (72) to Germany which consumes about twice as much as Japan (87 kg per person).

In conclusion, the report shows that the Asian countries have similar consumption numbers for both coffee and meat.

Pie chart

How to start

"The pie charts compare… (*what, who, when, where*). It can be clearly seen that … (describe the most noticeable feature)."

Vocabulary

When describing a pie chart, write about **the highest (significant, lowest) percentage, the majority (minority), the greatest (smallest) proportion, the lowest number, the most (least) popular (common) item**, etc.

If there is a piece representing 25%, you could write "**a quarter**", 50% - "**a half**", 75% - "**three quarters**".

How to describe and compare pie charts

Describe and compare the pieces one by one.

If a certain piece is two or three times bigger than another, you could write "**twice (three times) as many** Xs were used **as** Ys".

Another idea is to write "**X is much more (or considerably less) common than Y**".

Pie chart sample task

You should spend about 20 minutes on this task.

The charts below describe books sales of Famous Book Store in 2001.

Write a report for a university tutor describing the information shown.

You should write at least 150 words.

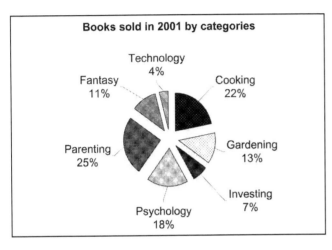

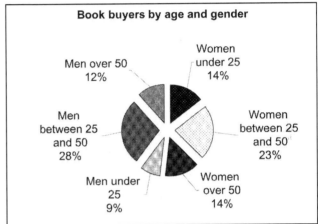

Sample answer:

The pie charts compare quantities of books of various categories sold to customers belonging to different age groups and gender during 2001 by Famous Book Store. It can be clearly seen that parenting books are the most popular and that the biggest proportion of books was sold to men between the ages of 25 and 50.

The two dominant categories, parenting (25 %) and cooking (22 %) are followed very closely by psychology, with only 4 percent less sales than for cooking books. Sales of fantasy and gardening literature recorded much smaller figures, 11 and 13 percent respectively. Books on Technology or Investment were the two least popular categories, with only seven percent of sales being on books about Investment and 4 percent on books on Technology.

Most of the books were sold to women and men from 25 to 50 years old (23 and 28 percent respectively). Sales figures amongst women older than 50 or younger than 25 as well as among men over 50 were very similar, 12 and 14 percent. Only 9 % of the books were purchased by men under 25.

Table

How to start

"The table compares… (*what, who, when, where*). It can be clearly seen that … (describe the most noticeable trend/feature)."

Vocabulary

The vocabulary is the same as for all previous figures. If a time period or date is not mentioned, assume the present.

How to select and group information

The table you receive usually has a lot of categories. It is presented to you that way *intentionally,* to make describing all the categories in 20 minutes impossible.

When you analyze a table, go row by row (or column by column) and look for the highest or the lowest numbers. It will help you find the categories you can **contrast** (by describing the **differences** between them).

If similar numbers appear in rows/columns – that's an opportunity for you to **compare** them (by describing the **similarities** between them).

You must learn to group information and describe groups of categories rather than just discarding the information. You can do this by noticing similar trends and grouping them together.

Table sample task

You should spend about 20 minutes on this task.

The table below describes victims by age group and offence category in Venezuela, 1999.

Write a report for a university lecturer describing the information shown.

You should write at least 150 words.

Age group\Offence	Murder	Negligence	Kidnapping	Robbery	Blackmail
0-14	14	39	110	523	4
15-24	25	4	56	4558	46
25-44	72	0	48	3312	89
45-64	38	2	16	1067	76
65+	13	9	3	220	8
Total victims	162	54	233	9680	223

Sample answer:

The table shows statistics of people in five age groups who became victims of various crimes in Venezuela in 1999. It can be clearly seen that robbery was the most common type of offence across all of the age groups.

The largest numbers of citizens were victims of either robbery or kidnapping, with over 4500 and 56 cases respectively for people over 15 and under 24 years old. These numbers reduce though by 25% (to 3312 and 48 respectively) as we move to age group 25 to 44 and reduce even more for ages 45 - 64, dropping to 1067 cases of robbery and 16 kidnappings. Figures for blackmail and murder victims show a very similar tendency to increase as we move from the 0-14 to the 25-44 age group, where they peak at 89 and 72 respectively.

Another noticeable feature is that the majority of the victims belonged to ages from 15 up to 64 for all kinds of offences, with the exceptions of negligence and kidnapping, where most of the victims belonged to the 0-14 age group.

Process

How to start

"The flow chart/diagram describes/reveals the procedures of / for …"

Vocabulary

When describing a process, explain the sequence of stages/actions and use words like: **firstly (secondly, thirdly), to begin with, then, after that, in addition, otherwise, at the same time (concurrently, simultaneously), finally**.

How to describe a process

Describe *every* stage of the process one by one, connect the stages by using linking words from the Vocabulary section (**firstly, then, finally, etc**), and mention whether or not there are stages that are being performed at the same time. You should also notice alternative stages (either stage A or B is performed). The main task here is to describe, not compare or contrast. Use **present simple passive** ("the letter is written" or "the research is conducted"). A conclusion paragraph is not necessary.

Process sample task

You should spend about 20 minutes on this task.

The diagram on the following page shows how online purchases are made.

Describe the process of online purchase.

You should write at least 150 words.

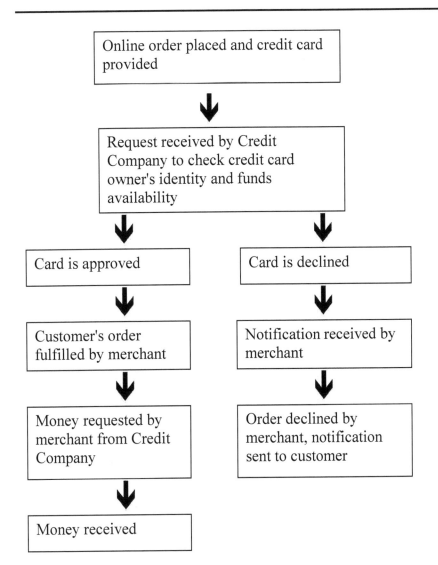

Sample answer:

The flow chart shows the detailed process of making a purchase online, including the actions of the customer, merchant and Credit Company.

First, the online order is placed together with the credit card number to enable the required funds to be withdrawn. Then a request to check the validity of the credit card (by checking that the customer is its real owner) and sufficiency of funds is received by the Credit Company. As a result, the credit card is either approved or denied by the company.

If the credit card is approved, the customer's order is fulfilled by the merchant. After that, the purchase amount is requested by the merchant from the Credit Company and finally, money is received by the merchant.

Alternatively, in cases when the credit card is denied by the Credit Company, notification is sent to the merchant advising them not to supply the goods. Next, the order is declined by the merchant and after that notification is sent to the customer.

Plan / map

How to start

"The map / plan / diagram describes / shows / indicates / illustrates … (*what/where/when*). It is clear / evident that … (describe the most noticeable feature or change)."

Vocabulary

When comparing maps, use words such as **north (to the north of…/ on the northerly side) / south / east / west** to describe locations of places. Remember to mention distances (**a long distance from / near / in the same area**). Look at the maps and try to find which facilities and buildings have been **replaced / relocated / built / constructed / demolished / knocked down / reduced or enlarged in size / extended.**

When comparing plans (of buildings, sites, etc) you can describe positions of places using words such as **next to / in front of / at the back of / across (the hall) / down the corridor / upstairs / above / downstairs / opposite / on the ground / first / second floor**. It is easier to describe where something is located in relation to a starting point: "**to the left of** the entrance / **directly opposite the** lobby / **across the hall from** the lift".

How to compare plans / maps

In the introduction paragraph you should rephrase the task statement using synonyms and then write a sentence about the most noticeable changes.

In the body paragraphs you should describe the changes that already occurred (if one map describes the past and the other – the present) or the changes that will occur (if one map describes the present and the other – the future). It may be necessary to mention the initial locations of buildings / trees / structures / rooms / facilities first, in order to explain later how they have changed or will change.

In the conclusion paragraph be brief and summarize the main changes in one sentence.

Plan / map sample task

You should spend about 20 minutes on this task.

The map on the next page shows the changes to Lakeside Holiday Park following its redevelopment in 2014.

Summarize the information by selecting and reporting the main features and make comparisons where relevant.

You should write at least 150 words.

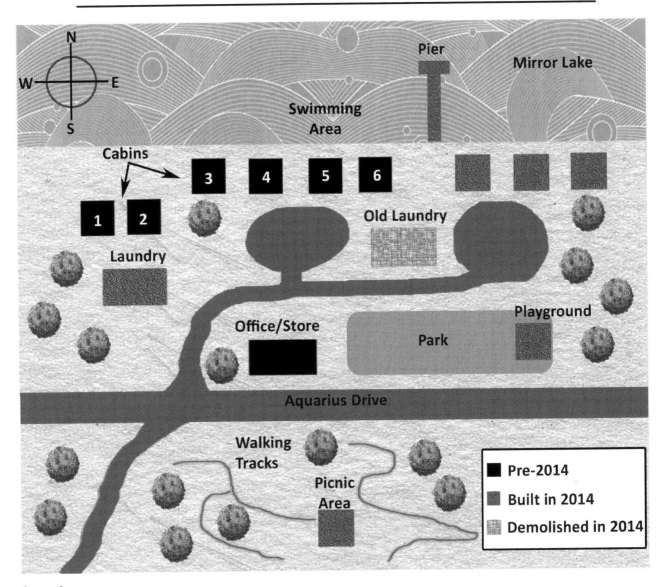

Sample answer:

The map illustrates the transformation of Lakeside Holiday Village as a result of redevelopment. It is clear that more accommodation is now available and the range of tourist facilities has increased.

The map shows that three new cabins have been constructed in 2014 to the east of the previously existing six cabins along the beach. Children can play at a new playground that has been built on the east side of the park. A new picnic area to the south of Aquarius Drive has been added for village guests to relax in after some walking along the nature trails.

A pier has been constructed to the east of the swimming area, between the two groups of cabins, old and new. This facilitates boating and fishing in Mirror Lake. The old laundry building that was located between two car parks has been demolished and replaced with a new laundry in a more discreet location, behind Cabins #1 and #2.

Overall, the 2014 redevelopment allows more guests to stay at the resort and their holiday activities are now more varied.

Practice, practice, practice!

I believe that practicing in writing is a must. Use the following topics to practice writing reports as much as you can. This will also help you understand better how to **group** the information in case you have to - for example when you are given a table or 2 graphs.

To view some sample answers visit the website below:
http://www.ielts-blog.com/ielts-writing-samples-essays-letters-reports/

Single line graph tasks

Practice task 1.

You should spend about 20 minutes on this task.

The graph on the right describes rainfall statistics for Somecountry.

Write a report for a university tutor describing the information shown.

You should write at least 150 words.

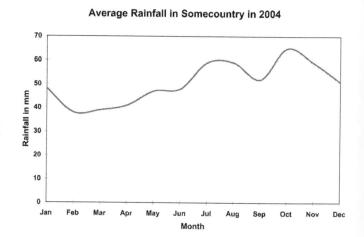

Practice task 2.

You should spend about 20 minutes on this task.

The graph on the right gives information on wages of Somecountry over a ten-year period.

Write a report for a university tutor describing the information shown.

You should write at least 150 words.

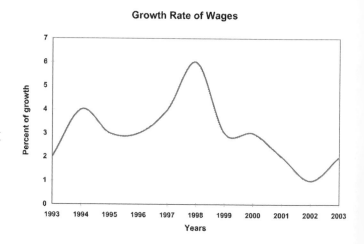

Double line graph tasks

Practice task 1.

You should spend about 20 minutes on this task.

The graph on the right shows how prices of "high-tech gadgets" changed over time in Somecountry.

Write a report for a university tutor describing the information shown.

You should write at least 150 words.

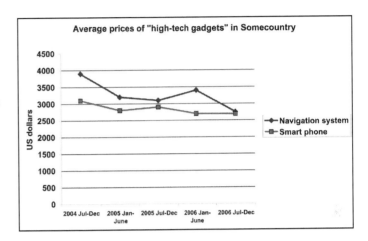

Practice task 2.

You should spend about 20 minutes on this task.

The graph on the right describes average house prices in Sometown in 2005.

Write a report for a university tutor describing the information shown.

You should write at least 150 words.

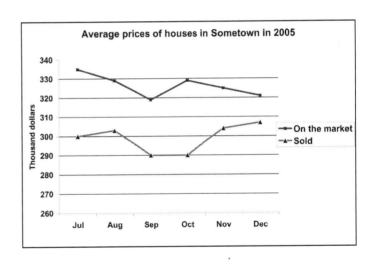

Bar graph tasks

Practice task 1.

You should spend about 20 minutes on this task.

The graph on the right shows the way people of Somecountry invested their money during the years 2001 - 2006.

Write a report for a university tutor describing the information shown.

You should write at least 150 words.

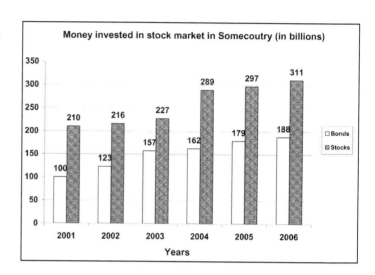

Practice task 2.

You should spend about 20 minutes on this task.

The graph on the right shows annual water usage (in millions of cubic meters) by industry in Somecountry.

Write a report for a university tutor describing the information shown.

You should write at least 150 words.

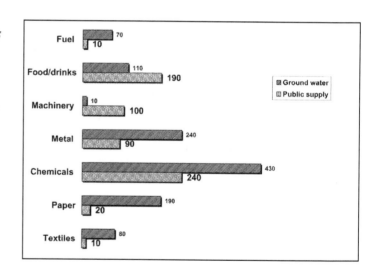

Pie chart task

You should spend about 20 minutes on this task.

The chart on the right describes results of a public opinion poll, where people were asked to name the most important place smoking should be banned from.

Write a report for a university tutor describing the information shown.

You should write at least 150 words.

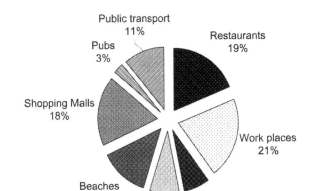

Where people think smoking should be banned

Pie chart/bar graph mixed task

You should spend about 20 minutes on this task.

The diagrams below contain information regarding percentages of people occupied in various types of position in 1999 and 2001. Write a report for a university tutor describing the information shown.

You should write at least 150 words.

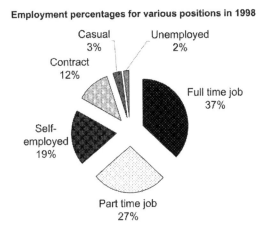

Employment percentages for various positions in 1998

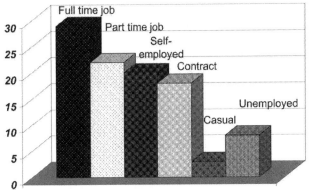

Employment percentages for various positions in 2001

Table tasks

Practice task 1.

You should spend about 20 minutes on this task.

The table below describes the percentages of home-schooled students in SomeCountry in 1999-2004. Write a report for a university lecturer describing the information shown.

You should write at least 150 words.

Grade/Year	1999	2000	2001	2002	2003	2004
Kindergarten	2.4	2.5	2.6	2.7	2.7	2.9
Grades 1- 2	1.5	1.2	1.3	1.5	1.8	2.1
Grades 3- 4	1.6	1.7	1.8	1.9	2.1	2.2
Grades 5- 6	1.5	1.3	1.3	1.6	2.1	2.6
Grades 7- 8	1.6	1.6	1.6	2.2	2.4	2.5

Practice task 2.

You should spend about 20 minutes on this task.

The table below describes the number of students studying foreign languages in SomeCountry in 2000-2005. Write a report for a university lecturer describing the information shown.

You should write at least 150 words.

Grade/Year	2000	2001	2002	2003	2004	2005
German	1811	1678	1717	1563	1325	1121
French	896	791	723	699	711	687
Spanish	1889	1987	2131	2278	2390	2453
Russian	20	25	27	24	30	26
Japanese	32	34	31	33	32	35

Process diagram task

You should spend about 20 minutes on this task.

The flowchart below explains how laundry is handled. Using information from the flowchart describe the laundry process.

You should write at least 150 words.

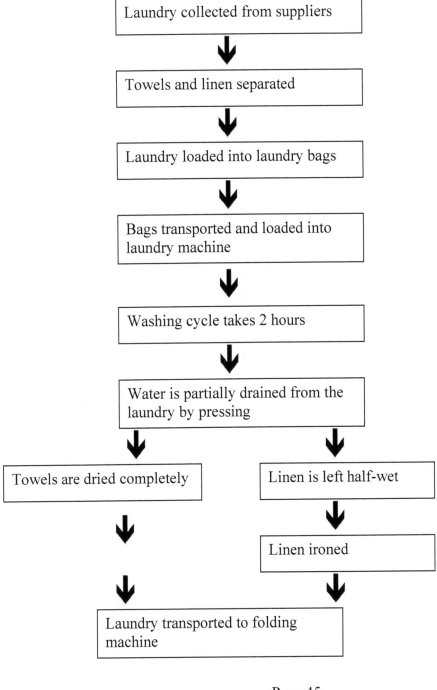

Plan / map task

You should spend about 20 minutes on this task.

The diagrams below show the current ground floor plan of a museum and the proposed changes to its layout. Summarize the information by selecting and reporting the main features, and make comparisons where relevant.

You should write at least 150 words.

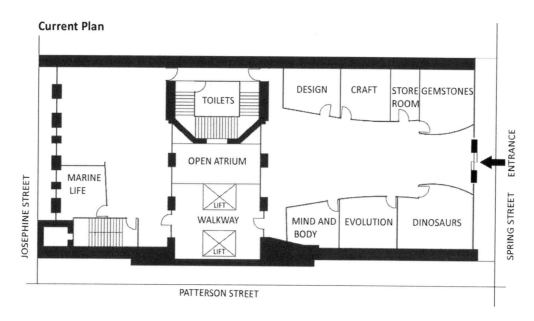

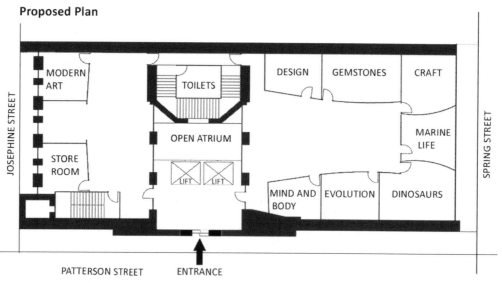

Tips for Writing Task 2 - Essay

You don't have to be a writer to write a good essay. This task may look even harder than the report, but it is only a first impression. Just follow the rules, keep the right structure, use some "smart" words and practice a little. This way you can easily reach a level, where no matter what topic they give you, after 40 minutes you turn out a beautiful 2-page essay and walk out of the room with a huge smile on your face.

Structure

Every essay should have this exact structure: **introduction**, **body** and **conclusion**.
It is very important because your grade is affected by it. The introduction usually takes one paragraph, the body - two or three paragraphs and the conclusion - one paragraph.

Essay topics - 3 different kinds

There are only 3 kinds of essay topics in IELTS, let's call them **A, H, S**.

Topic type "**A**" presents an **Argument** and you need to explore pros and cons, reasons for and against, while you support only one side.

Topic type "**H**" present a **Hidden argument**. These topics usually ask "To what extent …?", "In what way…?", "How has something changed…?"

Topic type "**S**" present a **Situation** and you need to explore **reasons** why it is what it is, assume what will happen in the future and suggest solutions to problems, if required.

The following **examples** demonstrate the differences between topics of A, H or S kind:

A: "Modern society benefits greatly from computer technology. However, becoming more dependent on computers has its disadvantages. Discuss the threats of computers."
Here the 2 sides of the argument are the advantages and disadvantages of computers.

H: "To what extent should television participate in our children's education?"
What they **really** ask here is whether the television should educate the children or not.

S: "As a result of tourism many unique places in the world are being damaged or even destroyed. Why is this happening? What are some possible solutions to this problem?"
Here you can see the description of a situation and you have to write what you think about it.

Essay of A(rgument) kind

1. **The introduction** paragraph must clearly state the argument, both sides of it. Do not simply copy the topic from the instructions, write it in **other** words. Don't give your opinion, save it for later.

2. **Body** paragraphs (at least 2) must refer to each side of the argument. Write the first paragraph about the side you disagree with. The side you do agree with should be in the **last** body paragraph, because this way it naturally leads to the conclusion.

3. **The conclusion** paragraph should contain a summary of the points you were making. Never mind if the paragraph turns out to be short, the important thing is that you kept the structure of the essay.

Essay of H(idden Argument) kind

1. **The introduction** paragraph must define the question. You need to reveal the hidden argument. Rewrite the topic, so it will say what it **really** means:
   from "to what extent something affects…?" **to** "Does something affect…?"
   from "in what way something contributes?" **to** "does something contribute?"
   from "how does something influence…?" **to** "does something influence …?
   Now it is an argument with two sides, and you write an essay of kind "**A**".

Essay of S(ituation) kind

1. **The introduction** paragraph must state the situation and explain it. Don't give your opinion here.

2. **Body** paragraphs (at least 2) should describe reasons that have led to the situation being like it is now. Each paragraph should talk about one reason.

3. **The conclusion** paragraph should summarize the key points of the essay. If the task requires suggesting a solution to a problem, recommendations, advice - this is the place for it. If your opinion is required - you should also give it in the conclusion paragraph.

General suggestions

- Write on the given topic directly, don't slide to another theme.

- Write in general, not about your personal experiences, but about what is going on in the world.

- Read the task instructions and write about every little thing that is requested. If the task requires suggesting a solution - do it.
  Don't forget to give recommendations or advice, if requested.

Baby Steps through the essay

After you have read all that, you still have no idea how to start writing.
So let's do it together:

 **First Step**

Read and classify the question. You need to decide what kind of topic you have got, an A, H or S. It will affect the way you plan your essay.

Example:

"Home schooling belongs to the past and is unacceptable in modern society. To what extent do you agree or disagree with this statement?
Use your own knowledge and experience and support your arguments with examples and relevant evidence"

We can clearly see a hidden argument here. By revealing the real meaning of the topic we get "Is home schooling acceptable in modern society?" This way it becomes an "A" topic, an argument with 2 sides - for and against home education.

Second Step

Here you need to come up with ideas, thoughts and opinions on the given topic. The best way to do it is to think of some *main* ideas and then to write everything you can think of regarding those ideas. In case you are working on an essay of an "A" or "H" kind, you need to think about ideas for and against the topic. If you are working on an essay of kind "S" - you need to think about the reasons for the situation to be the way it is.

Example:

Let's say that after some thinking you came up with the following ideas, and your opinion is **against** education at home.

For	Against
parents know their children	no scientific approach (like associative learning)
learning is more enjoyable	not every parent is capable
children feel safe	parents forgot the material

Now you should think about what goes where in your essay. On the same draft paper where you have written the ideas, group them and decide which paragraph will describe which idea. If the topic is an argument (type A), remember to put the side you don't agree with first and the side you do agree with second. Think about how to move from one paragraph to another. There should be a connective logical sentence that drives you towards the next paragraph's topic.

Example:

Parents know their children	1st body paragraph	side you don't agree with
Learning is more enjoyable	1st body paragraph	
Children feel safe	1st body paragraph	
no scientific approach	2nd body paragraph	side you do agree with
associative learning	2nd body paragraph	
not every parent is capable	3rd body paragraph	side you do agree with

Third Step

It is time to write the answer. According to the plan you have made, start writing the essay. The first sentence of the introduction gives the main idea of the essay, either presenting sides of the argument or describing a situation. The last sentence of the introduction should naturally lead into the first paragraph of the body. Remember to keep the paragraph structure and to connect paragraphs so that one leads to another.

Important! Try to start body paragraphs with a linking word (like However, Therefore, Moreover, Nevertheless, etc.). It raises your score.

Example:

This is an essay written according to the ideas you came up with. The ideas are in bold font for easier understanding.

Everything has two sides and home schooling is not an exception. In the past it seemed like the most natural way of educating children, but today many people criticize it.

*We must acknowledge that **parents know their children best**. That gives them a good chance of knowing how to make their child understand certain concepts. Using their child's interests, parents can make the process of **learning more enjoyable** and effective. In addition, being at home makes a **child feel safe**, which contributes to his ability to concentrate on studying.*

Nevertheless, many people believe that teaching should be done by professionals.
*There are many proven **scientific approaches** that produce good results and without those techniques, parents who teach their kids at home have no chance of success. **Associative learning** is a good example of such a technique. Showing the child images while learning the alphabet (apple for "a", boy for "b") makes him or her remember the letters faster and easier.*

*In addition, **not every parent is capable** of teaching his or her child at home because the blind cannot lead the blind. Parents cannot teach children something they don't know themselves, and let's face it - not all of us have a profound knowledge of history or geography even on a school textbook level. Eventually, even those mums and dads who succeeded at school could **forget material** with the passage of time.*

In conclusion, I have more trust in the abilities and experience of professional teachers than I do in my own.

And finally - **read the essay carefully from the beginning and check it for errors**.

40 minutes? Not enough!

Hardly anyone can get their first essays done on time. So don't be disappointed if it takes you an hour or even longer. First try to get used to the Baby Steps process that I explained earlier. After a little bit of practice, you will start writing essays faster and faster, and finally you will reach your goal - an essay in 40 minutes. You should work with a clock all the time - this is the only way for you to monitor your progress.

Helpful phrases

Usually people who don't read and write in English every day have trouble expressing themselves in an essay. So I enclose here a list of phrases to help you write more elegant sentences.

Phrases to show two sides of an argument

- "Some people prefer …. Those who disagree point out that…"
- "We must acknowledge … Nevertheless, …"
- "No one can deny … However, …"
- "Many people hold the opinion… Others, however, disagree…"
- "Although it is hard to compete with …, some people still prefer …"

Phrases for adding a linked point

- "Not only…, but…"
- "Also"
- "Furthermore,"
- "In addition,"
- "Moreover,"

Phrases to contrast with what was written before

- "Although…"
- "However,"
- "Nevertheless,"
- "Even if…"
- "In spite of"
- "On the other hand"

Phrases for examples

- "For example,"
- "For instance,"
- "In particular,"
- "…, such as"
- "To illustrate …"

Phrases for results

- "As a result"
- "Therefore"
- "Thus"
- "So"
- "Eventually"

Phrases for conclusion

- "Lastly,"
- "Finally,"
- "To conclude with,"
- "In short,"
- "In conclusion,"

Practice, practice, practice!

My advice would be to practice on essays as much as you can. Your goal is to be able to write an essay of 250 words in 40 minutes on any given topic. The topic doesn't matter, the important thing is that you know and implement the techniques you've learned.

So for those of you who don't take chances, the following list of topics is similar to those you will get in IELTS. Practice with a clock and count the number of words.

To view some sample answers visit the website below:
http://www.ielts-blog.com/ielts-writing-samples-essays-letters-reports/

Topic 1   *(Hint: Argument)*

You should spend about 40 minutes on this task.

Even though globalization affects the world's economics in a very positive way, its negative side should not be forgotten. Discuss.

You should write at least 250 words.

Topic 2   *(Hint: Hidden Argument)*

You should spend about 40 minutes on this task.

Some people say that the education system is the only critical factor in the development of a country. To what extent do you agree or disagree with this statement?

You should write at least 250 words.

Topic 3   *(Hint: Argument)*

You should spend about 40 minutes on this task.

Dieting can change a person's life for the better or ruin one's health completely. What is your opinion?

You should write at least 250 words.

Topic 4   *(Hint: Hidden Argument)*

You should spend about 40 minutes on this task.

Education in financial management should be a mandatory component of the school program. To what extent do you agree or disagree with this statement?

You should write at least 250 words.

Topic 5   *(Hint: Argument)*

You should spend about 40 minutes on this task.

The best way to reduce the number of traffic accidents is to raise the age limit for younger drivers and to lower the age limit for elderly ones. Do you agree?

You should write at least 250 words.

Topic 6   *(Hint: Situation)*

You should spend about 40 minutes on this task.

Obesity was once considered a disease of adults; however, it is becoming increasingly common among children. Why do you think this is happening? What can be done to help children stay healthy?

You should write at least 250 words.

Tips for the Speaking test

Finally, we have reached the fun part of IELTS. Many people agree that the secret of success in the Speaking test is being a confident and creative person. Does it mean that others will fail? Not at all! This test is **PREDICTABLE**. Use the following tips to prepare yourself for what's coming and the confidence will come.

What are they looking for?

If you know what is important to IELTS examiners, it improves your chances of success. These guidelines refer to every part of the Speaking test. Stick to them and you will satisfy your examiner.

- Speak without long pauses (when you are trying to think of something to say)

- Understand what the examiner asks you and confirm that by answering accordingly.

- Demonstrate how many "smart" words you know.

- Use all the tenses when you speak - past, present, future - and use them correctly.

- Pronounce the words correctly. For example the word "culture" should sound like "kolcher", not "kultur".

- Important! Accent has nothing to do with pronunciation, so it will not affect your score.

Keep it simple!

This tip refers to the whole Speaking test. Don't start long and complicated sentences if you don't know how to finish them! Keep your sentences simple, and words - understandable. If you make a grammatical error - it's ok to correct yourself, but don't overdo it, you must sound fluent.

When you hear a question, your mind automatically develops an image with the answer.
You can describe this image in your own language, but when you start to describe it in English, suddenly you don't have enough words in your vocabulary. So try to think of what part of that image you **can** describe, do it and stop there. Don't let yourself show what words you don't know by saying incomplete sentences.

Interview

The first part of the Speaking test is the Interview. You enter the room, see the examiner, say "Good afternoon!" and smile. He or she asks to see your passport and invites you to sit down. If he/she offers to shake your hand - do it, otherwise - don't.
Your body language is important here, it must show that you are relaxed and confident. When you are talking, try to make eye contact with the examiner as much as you can.

During the interview the examiner asks you questions about yourself, your work, studies, parents, brothers/sisters, pets, etc. Your answer to each question should consist of one or two sentences; try not to answer with just "yes" or "no". After all it's your English they want to hear.

This is an easy task to prepare for. Read the following questions and answers carefully, and you will get a very clear picture of what will happen.

Possible questions and answers

1. **Where do you come from?**
   I live in Smallville. It is a big city /small town located in the south of NeverNeverLand.

2. **What is your home like?**
   I rent an apartment. We have two bedrooms, one living room, one kitchen and of course one restroom. The apartment is not very big, about 70 square meters.

3. **What do you like or dislike about your home?**
   The advantage is that my accommodation has lots of sunlight from the windows. And the disadvantage is that it is noisy because the centre of the city is nearby.

4. **Tell me about your family.**
   I have a mother, a father and a brother. My mother is a social worker, my father is a civil engineer and my brother is a student.

5. **Tell me about your job.**
   Well, I work for a big firm /small company named BananaSoft. It is located in Smallville. My job title is Software Designer.

6. **Is there anything you dislike about your job?**
   Normally, I enjoy my job very much. But sometimes my boss gives me boring assignments, which I don't like at all.

7. What are your plans for the future?

I would like to improve my English first and then find another job with a better salary.

8. What type of transport do you use most?

There are 2 types of transport that I use: I either drive my car or take the bus.

9. Do you like reading?

Yes I do. I enjoy reading very much. Usually, I read every other day of the week.

10. What do you most like to read?

I enjoy reading newspapers, magazines and of course my favorite fantasy books.

11. What kind of television programs do you watch?

Well, my favorite channel is Some TV Channel. I find it very interesting and educational.

12. Tell me about a film you have seen recently

I saw "Some New Movie" a week ago. It is a comedy and I like comedies. This one has some silly jokes but other than that I enjoyed it.

13. Do you have a pet?

Yes I do. I have a dog named Richy. He is 4 years old.

14. What kind of food do you like?

I prefer Asian cooking, mostly Chinese. My favorite dish is noodles with vegetables.

15. How often do you go shopping?

Well, I don't like shopping, so I do it only when I have to.

16. What is your favorite festival and why?

I like October Fest. It's a German festival that starts in late September and ends in October. People drink lots of beer at October Fest and that is why I like it.

17. How do people celebrate this festival?

Well, they build pavilions and stands that sell beer and all kinds of food, a lot of bands are playing there. People from all around Europe come to celebrate the October Fest dressed in traditional, German clothes.

Speech

After you have finished the Interview, the examiner will hand you a card with 3 or 4 questions on it. Usually the card asks you to describe a place, an event or a situation from your experience. You have 1 minute to prepare a little speech that answers all of the questions on a card. You also receive a sheet of paper and a pen to write your notes.

The speech should take between one and two minutes. In the end, the examiner might ask you a couple of additional questions.

The tricky part here is to know when 2 minutes have passed. You need to get a feeling what is it like to talk for 2 minutes. My suggestion is to practice at home with a clock, recording yourself while you are speaking on a particular topic. You can use MP3 players that can record. This way you can evaluate your own speech without any help from other people.

Example

Let's take the following topic card and see what kind of speech you should give:

> Describe a journey you went on. You should include in your answer:
>
> • Where you went on your journey
>
> • Why you went to this particular place
>
> • What did you do and with whom
>
> • Whether you enjoyed your journey or not and why

Possible answer:

> "I would like to tell you about a journey I went on a year ago. My wife and I took a trip to Holland.
>
> Both of us wanted to visit Amsterdam very much because we had seen pictures and heard stories from friends about how beautiful and wonderful it is. So finally we bought plane tickets, booked a hotel, packed our bags and our trip began.
>
> We spent a lot of time before our holiday researching all the interesting places to visit and all the sights to see. So we went to the Amstell Beer museum, took a romantic sunset cruise along the canals, drove to Volendam, a really pretty, small fishing village, and visited a cheese farm. Every evening we took long walks along the canals, stopping to rest in small gardens, which Amsterdam has a lot of. Street artists were performing everywhere and a lot of people came to watch.
>
> We enjoyed everything we did very much and especially being together in such a beautiful country. Having my wife by my side on this trip made it even more fun."

Practice, practice, practice

I have included here a selection of cards for you to practice on. Choose a card, prepare for 1 minute, writing down the points you will speak about. When you start speaking, try not to get in trouble - don't use words unless you know what they mean, don't use long complicated sentences where you get lost in words. Try to speak simply and make it sound interesting.

Describe a book that has had a major influence on you.
You should include in your answer:

- What the book's title is and who wrote it
- How you first heard of it
- What the book is about
- Why it has played such an important role in your life

Describe your favorite restaurant. You should include in your answer:

- Where it is located in the city
- What it looks like inside and outside
- What kind of food is served there
- What makes this restaurant so special to you and others

Describe a museum you visited. You should mention in your answer:

- Where this museum is situated
- Why people visit the museum
- What it looked like
- Why you liked this museum

Describe a conflict you once had at work. You should mention:

- The nature of the conflict
- Why the conflict occurred
- What you felt at the time of the conflict
- What you had to do to resolve it

Discussion

In the third sub-part of the test you have a discussion with the examiner. The topic is somehow related to the one from section two, but it is about ideas that are more abstract. Your job is to express and justify an opinion. It is called a discussion, but in reality *you are the one who does most of the talking.*

To give you an idea of what it will be like, here is a card you might get in part 2 of the Speaking test:

Describe a good friend of yours. You should say

- Where and when you met
- What you do together
- What you like about him/her, and
- Why she/he is a good friend of yours

Then in the third sub-part of the Speaking test the examiner may ask you this kind of questions:

- What sort of person would you not be able to have as a good friend?
- What do you value and not value in people?
- Can people, opposite in personality, be good friends?
- What do children think about friendship? What about adults? Compare them.
- What do you think of friendship formed through the internet? What good and bad aspects does it have?

Have an opinion!

Now that you have got the idea, how do you prepare for this kind of test?
Well, you need to have an opinion on a wide range of different topics.

I include here a list of some of the most common topics for you to think about.
Just go over them, think of what you have to say on those issues and think of which words you will use. Then record yourself saying a couple of sentences on each of the topics and listen to what comes out. Think of what you could have done better. This should get you ready for the Discussion part.

You can view the latest topics from real IELTS exams in the website below:
http://www.ielts-blog.com/category/recent-ielts-exams

And this is a summary of topics for you to think about:

<u>General topics</u>

- o The main industry in your country now, how it will develop in the future.
- o Effects of pollution on ecology.
- o Popular forms of transport in your country.
- o How to improve public transport.
- o How your country has been improved.
- o The city you are living in, its advantages and disadvantages.
- o Your country's weather, main seasons.
- o Your country's animals, in what ways they are used.
- o A piece of equipment that you consider very important, why, how you started to use it.
- o Computers - their advantages and disadvantages, whether people of different sexes and ages use them more or less.
- o Food in restaurants, why and when we eat there, what are the pros and cons of eating in a restaurant.
- o Celebrities in your country.
- o Idols - who chooses them, who copies them, etc.
- o A favorite holiday in your country.

<u>About yourself</u>

- o How do you like spending your time?
- o Favorite movies (films), do you watch them on TV or in cinema.
- o Would you like to act in movies? Why not?
- o Where you like to spend your vacation.
- o Study or work, where, what do you like most about your job, what do you dislike about your job?
- o Your future plans.
- o Your hobbies.
- o Do you think free time is important and why?
- o What did you study at university?
- o Which subject is your favorite?
- o Which subject don't you like?
- o What do you want to do in the future?
- o Your favorite food.
- o The greatest success in your life.
- o Design of your apartment, likes, dislikes, why?
- o The room you like most, what you do there most, what it looks like.
- o Your favorite sportsmen.
- o Favorite TV program.
- o Most interesting time in your life.

Things that were important in your life

- An important song.
- An important book - what was it about, how did it influence you?
- A doll or some other toy, who gave it to you, on what occasion, what did you do with it?

Friends

- Who is your best friend?
- Where and when did you meet?
- What do you like the best about him/her?
- What have you done together? Explain the reasons why you have a strong friendship.
- What do children think about friendship? What about adults? Compare them.
- What sort of person would you not be able to have as a good friend?
- Can people, opposite in personality, be good friends?
- What do you value and not value in people?
- Friendship through the Internet, good and bad sides

Household

- Who does the shopping?
- Where do you like to shop and when?
- What do you shop for?
- Who does the housework, which work is the most important, why?

Traveling

- How can a visitor travel in my country?
- How did your grandparents travel in the past?
- Will the travel method change in the future?
- Traveling in a group compared with traveling on your own.
- What kinds of holidays exist?
- Where people prefer to go on vacation.
- Developments that have a positive effect on the growth of tourism.

Toys

- Why boys and girls chose different toys.
- Why toys are good for kids.
- Negative influence of toys, educational side of toys.

Music

- What kind of music do you like?
- Why we should teach music to our kids.

What if …?

It can happen that the examiner asks you a question and you don't have a clue what he/she is talking about. Don't panic! Just say:

- I am not sure what you mean, could you be more specific?
- Could you repeat the question, please?

If you don't have a ready answer and you are trying to borrow some time, say:

- Well, I've never thought about that, but I would say that…
- Well, it is not a simple question.

If they ask for your opinion, you can start by saying:

- In my opinion…
- I think that…
- Well, if you ask me, …
- When it comes to me, I …

You will probably have to speak in present, past and future tenses. When asked to speak about the future, say:

- I am sure that (something will/won't happen)
- It is likely/unlikely that (some event will / won't occur)

Leave a good impression

FINALLY!!! When leaving the room after the interview, look the examiner in the eyes, smile and simply say: *"Thank you for your time. Good bye"*.

Isn't life great? :)

Pocket tips

Listening
- Read instructions.
- Guess what is missing: is it a word, a place, a name, a number, how many?
- Divide questions into groups.
- Listen for details.
- Anything said loud and clear could be an answer, whispered - not an answer.
- Repetition and dictation - answer.
- Multiple choices - use T/F/NG method to eliminate all choices but one.
- Gap fills - look around the gaps for clues (Bad grammar = wrong answer).
- Traps: Change of mind, generalization, explicit answers.
- Copy answers: just the letter, not the circle,
  just your answer, not the whole sentence.

Reading
- Read instructions
- Manage your time.
- Make a map.
- Easy questions first - complicated second.
- Look for keywords.
- Matching headings - use the map.
- T/F/NG: Clearly said = True
  - Opposite to what is said = False
  - Not what is said = Not Given
- Multiple Choices - use T/F/NG method to eliminate all choices but one.
- Gap fills - use the map to find where the answer is hiding.
- Don't make assumptions!
- Have time left - check your answers.

Speaking

Interview:	Be confident and relaxed
	Eye contact with the examiner
	Answer every question with at least 2 sentences
Speech:	Write down main points
	Speak simply - no big words if you aren't sure how to use them
	Make it sound interesting
Discussion:	Have an opinion on everything
	Any opinion is acceptable (no "good" or "bad" opinions)
	In the end, thank the examiner and shake hands

Writing: Reports

Single Line Graph
- Introduction: "The graph describes/shows/reveals … (what, who, when, where). It can be clearly seen that …(describe main trends)." Don't copy sentences from task!
- Notice distinctive features and describe them. Write about all the periods of time and about all the subjects of the graph. Never use bullets.
- Describing trends: rises (increases, climbs, goes up), falls (decreases, declines, drops, goes down, doesn't change (remains at the same level, maintains stability), peak, lowest point, speed of change: fast (rapidly, quickly) or slowly (gradually, steadily), order: rise was preceded by drop and followed by decline
- Time stamp and correct tense:
  Happened in the past ("Books sold in 2001") = use past simple
  Continued in the past ("The way people were spending money on apparel between 1999 and 2003") = use past continuous
  Happens in the present ("Recent unemployment figures") = use present simple or present continuous

---

Double Line Graph
- Introduction: "The graph compares … (what, who, when, where). It can be clearly seen that … (describe main trends of 2 graphs here).

- Describe first graph, write "similarly" if the second is alike or "in contrast" if it is different, then describe the other graph. Write about all the periods of time and about all the subjects of the graph. Compare peaks and lowest points of 2 graphs.

Bar Graph
- Introduction: for single bar graph:"The graph describes/shows/reveals … (what, who, when, where). It can be clearly seen that …(describe main trends)."
  For multiple bars graph: "The graph compares … (what, who, when, where). It can be clearly seen that … (describe main trends here)."

- If the axis of bar graph is a time scale - describe how graph's subject changes in time. Otherwise compare the bars differently - more, less, most, least, etc, by order of appearance. Never use bullets.

Table
- Introduction: "The table compares/describes/shows/reveals … (what, who, when, where). It can   be clearly seen that …(describe most noticeable trend)."

- Group information and describe groups of categories instead of throwing information away. Group categories with similar behavior.

Pie chart

- Introduction: "The pie chart(s) compare(s)…(what, who, when, where). It can be clearly seen that …(describe the most noticeable feature)."

- Describe and compare the pieces one by one, for example:
  "Twice (three times) as many Xs were used as Ys".
  "X is much more (or considerably less) common than Y"

- Vocabulary :
  highest (significant, lowest) percentage,
  greatest (smallest) proportion,
  lowest number,
  most (least) popular (common)

Process / Flow chart

- Introduction: "The flow chart/diagram describes/reveals the procedures of / for …"

- Describe every stage of the process one by one, don't break the sequence

- Connect stages by linking words: firstly (secondly, thirdly), to begin with, then, after that, in addition, otherwise, at the same time (concurrently, simultaneously), finally.

- Time stamp and correct tense:
  Use present simple passive ("the letter is written" or "the research is conducted").

- Conclusion paragraph is not necessary.

Writing: Essay

3 types of topics: Argument, Hidden argument, Situation

Plan for Argument and Hidden Argument topic type (5 paragraphs)

1. Introduction - 2 sides of the argument
2. Write about side you don't agree with
3. Write about side you do agree with
4. Write more about side you agree with
5. Conclusion - sum up, suggestions, solutions.

Plan for Situation topic type (5 paragraphs)

1. Introduction - define the situation
2. Write about reason # 1 for the situation
3. Write about reason # 2 for the situation
4. Write about reason # 3 for the situation
5. Conclusion - sum up, suggestions, solutions.

Study Plan

All the tips I have shared with you so far are priceless, but they will be worth even more if you use them while practicing. As I said before, there are those who study and don't pass, and there are those who don't study and pass. And then there are people like us - we study a little, and then ace the IELTS!

My advice is: if you have decided to take the IELTS test, give yourself a month of studying according to this plan and give IELTS your best shot right away! Don't wait, don't take long breaks between studying, give it your all - and the success will follow.

There follows a suggested study plan for 21 days that should help you get the best IELTS score you can with your current level of English. All of the IELTS tasks appear in equal proportion. You can change that by doing more of the tasks you feel weak at and removing some (not all!) of the tasks you feel strong at. Remember, it is important to practice in all the tasks and not concentrate just on the ones you fear most.

In this book I have included Writing 1 (report) and Writing 2 (essay) tasks, interview questions, topic cards and themes for the Speaking test. At the end of the book there is also a full IELTS-like practice test. Additional material for studying (audio files for the Listening test, texts for the Reading test, etc) can be found on the following very helpful internet sites:

For the Listening test:

http://ielts-blog.com/online-practice/ - choose course type (General/Academic), then click on a big square button that says "FREE"
http://www.ieltsgym.com/?id=FreeEnglishlessons - online exercises with answers
http://www.esl-lab.com/- for this one you will need a Real Audio Player
http://www.ieltsontrack.com/mini_test.php?module=1 - a test with a transcript

For the Reading test:

http://ielts-blog.com/online-practice/ - choose course type (General/Academic), then click on a big square button that says "FREE"
http://www.ieltsgym.com/?id=FreeEnglishlessons
http://www.examenglish.com/IELTS/IELTS_reading_2.htm
http://www.ieltsontrack.com/mini_test.php?module=2

For the Writing and Speaking tests:

http://www.ielts-blog.com/ielts-writing-samples-essays-letters-reports/
http://www.ielts-blog.com/category/recent-ielts-exams/

And of course there are many others, just look up the words "IELTS" and "forum" in any search engine. The internet moves so quickly, by the time you are reading this book there might be many new forums I have never heard of. If you find them or my links are not good any more - please let me know, I will update them and you will receive a FREE up-to-date copy of this book

Day	Tasks	Time	Remarks
1	Speaking Listening Writing 2 (type A)	30 minutes 30 minutes 60 minutes	Take a 5-10 minute break between tasks
2	Writing 1 (Single line) Listening Reading	30 minutes 30 minutes 60 minutes	Take a 5-10 minute break between tasks
3	Speaking Listening Writing 2 (type S)	30 minutes 30 minutes 60 minutes	Take a 5-10 minute break between tasks
4	Writing 1 (Double line) Listening Reading	30 minutes 30 minutes 60 minutes	Take a 5-10 minute break between tasks
5	Speaking Writing 2 (type A)	30 minutes 60 minutes	Take a 5-10 minute break between tasks
6	Writing 1 (Bar graph) Listening Reading	30 minutes 30 minutes 60 minutes	Take a 5-10 minute break between tasks
7	Speaking Writing 2 (type S)	30 minutes 60 minutes	Take a 5-10 minute break between tasks
8	Writing 1 (Pie chart) Listening Reading	30 minutes 30 minutes 60 minutes	Take a 5-10 minute break between tasks
9	Speaking Listening Writing 2 (type A)	30 minutes 30 minutes 60 minutes	Take a 5-10 minute break between tasks
10	Writing 1 (Table) Reading Listening	30 minutes 60 minutes 30 minutes	Take a 5-10 minute break between tasks
11	Speaking Writing 2 (type S) Reading	30 minutes 40 minutes 60 minutes	Take a 5-10 minute break between tasks

Day	Tasks	Time	Remarks
12	Writing 1 (Process diagram) Reading Listening	30 minutes 60 minutes 30 minutes	Take a 5-10 minute break between tasks
13	Speaking Listening Writing 2 (type A)	30 minutes 30 minutes 40 minutes	Take 5-10 minutes break between tasks
14	Writing 1 (Double line) Reading	30 minutes 60 minutes	Take 5-10 minutes break between tasks
15	Full IELTS test: Listening Reading Writing 1 Writing 2 Speaking	40 minutes 60 minutes 20 minutes 40 minutes 15 minutes	Don't take breaks, continue through the whole test
16	Listening Writing 2	30 minutes 40 minutes	Take 5-10 minutes break between tasks
17	Speaking Writing 2 (type S)	30 minutes 40 minutes	Take 5-10 minutes break between tasks
18	Writing 1 (Table) Reading Speaking	20 minutes 60 minutes 30 minutes	Take 5-10 minutes break between tasks
19	Speaking Writing 1 (Pie chart) Listening	30 minutes 20 minutes 30 minutes	Take 5-10 minutes break between tasks
20	Writing 2 (type A) Reading	40 minutes 60 minutes	Take 5-10 minutes break between tasks
21	Full IELTS test: Listening Reading Writing 1 Writing 2 Speaking	40 minutes 60 minutes 20 minutes 40 minutes 15 minutes	Don't take breaks, continue through the whole test

FULL IELTS PRACTICE TEST

ACADEMIC LISTENING PRACTICE TEST

Visit the following webpage to download the Listening Test recording:
http://www.ielts-blog.com/book-practice-test/

SECTION 1   Questions 1 – 10

Questions 1 – 5

Complete Apollo Car Rentals' new rental form below.
Write NO MORE THAN THREE WORDS AND/OR A NUMBER from the listening for each answer.

Apollo Car Rentals New Rental Form	
Example: Length of Rental	**5 days**
Client's Name	**(1)** _____ Anderson
Age	**(2)** _____
Address	28 Woodland Close, Hightown
Postcode	**(3)** _____
Mobile Telephone	07734 618 223
Payment Method	**(4)** _____
Rental Dates	21st - 25th May
Car Size	**(5)** _____
Price	£240

Questions 6 – 10

Answer the questions below. Use NO MORE THAN THREE WORDS AND/OR A NUMBER from the listening for each answer.

6   What will Carol find in the glove compartment to help her in case of an accident?
7   What's the fuel tank capacity of Carol's rental car?
8   Where is Carol going to leave her car when she's finished with it?
9   What does Ben give Carol for free?
10   How far is *The Haven* hotel from the airport?

SECTION 2   Questions 11 – 20

Questions 11 – 14

Complete the sentences below.

Use NO MORE THAN THREE WORDS from the listening for each answer.

11   The Youth Club's opening hours are from _____ p.m. to 11 p.m.
12   The _____ of six individuals is responsible for the administration of the Youth Club.
13   New _____ are always needed to help improve services, even for a short time.
14   A combination of membership, admittance fees, and help from the _____, individuals and local companies, make up the funding for the Youth Club.

Questions 15 – 20

Complete the table below.

Write NO MORE THAN TWO WORDS AND/OR A NUMBER from the listening for each answer.

Activity	When	Notes
The Homework Club	Weekday evenings From 4.00 p.m.	* 2 hours long * Quiet environment * 2 members of **(15)** _____ are always there
Basketball	Tuesdays and Thursdays 6 p.m. - 7.30 p.m.	* Takes place in the club's 2 sports halls * 2 coaches - 1 from the local pro team, the other from the local secondary school * Frequent **(16)** _____ are organized
Music Evenings	Tuesdays, Thursdays and Fridays 7 p.m. - 9 p.m.	* Come early as very popular * Free music studio * 3 local DJ's help out + local **(17)** _____ teach the children
Dramatic Arts	Mondays and Wednesdays 6.30 p.m. - 10 p.m.	* Volunteers teach drama and **(18)** _____ to the children * Regular performances held
Visits from the **(19)** _____	Periodic	* Talks and advice on alcohol, drugs, crime and other things * Children can ask questions
Overnight Hiking Trips	From time to time	* Skilled adults supervise * Children learn outdoor skills - camping, cooking food, use of **(20)** _____ and a compass * Children gain important character strengths

SECTION 3   Questions 21 – 30

Questions 21 – 26

Complete the student notes below on the second year linguistics course.

Write NO MORE THAN TWO WORDS from the listening for each answer.

The Second Year Linguistic Course

Delivered as lectures, supervision, essays and **(21)** _____ - attendance at all is compulsory.

The number of topics studied depends on which chosen.

Topics

Phonetics	* Study of practical, acoustic and clinical phonetics, speech perception and phonological theories. * Focus on connecting theory to practical speech, and data analysis, special focus on **(22)** _____. * Compulsory.

Clinical Linguistics	* Prepares students for work with communication problems in:
	   - **(23)** _____ with language or hearing problems.
	   - people who've had a stroke.

Onomastics	* The study of origins and development of English **(24)** _____. * Their special properties. * An enjoyable course. * Not the best for jobs, but there are possibilities in **(25)** _____ and advertising.
Sociolinguistics	* Taught by Professor Cotton. * The study of the relationship between people and society. * How the relationship causes **(26)** _____. * How age, geography, media and the language system influence speech.

Questions 27 - 30

Complete the flow chart that summarises the process of writing a dissertation.

Use NO MORE THAN ONE WORD from the listening for each answer.

The Dissertation Process

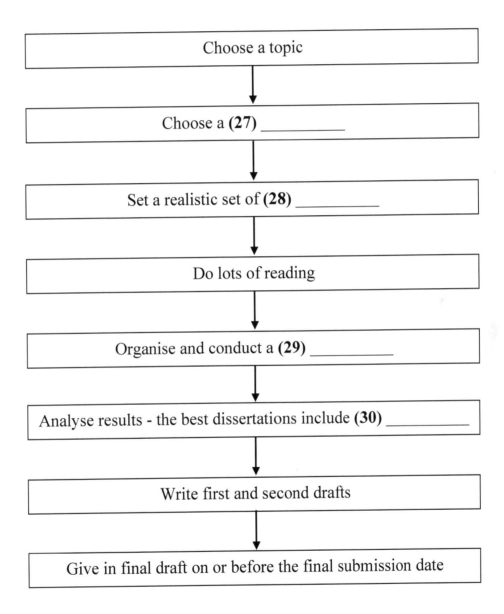

Choose a topic

↓

Choose a **(27)** _____

↓

Set a realistic set of **(28)** _____

↓

Do lots of reading

↓

Organise and conduct a **(29)** _____

↓

Analyse results - the best dissertations include **(30)** _____

↓

Write first and second drafts

↓

Give in final draft on or before the final submission date

SECTION 4 Questions 31 – 40

Questions 31 – 38

Complete the notes below. Use **NO MORE THAN TWO WORDS** from the listening for each answer.

Endangered Sharks in Australia

Out of 400 species of shark worldwide, 180 are in Australia in all coastal habitats, including even a few sharks in some **(31)** _____ habitats.

The two most endangered sharks in Australia are the grey nurse shark and speartooth shark - both are on the **(32)** _____ .

The Grey Nurse Shark	* 2 separate populations. * Not the man-eater its reputation gives - not usually dangerous unless provoked. * Often blamed for attacks because of its **(33)** _____ , which has led to lots of killing of the shark.
The Speartooth Shark	* Little research done due to lack of specimens, its rarity and confusion in the **(34)** _____ of it and other species. * Similar to northern river shark and the bull shark; the latter often shares the same environment for its **(35)** _____ . * Speartooth very vulnerable to exploitation. * Threats include fishing (commercial and recreational), netting and deterioration of its **(36)** _____ .

Beach Nets

Beach protecting shark nets lead to many shark deaths and are found in many countries affected by shark attacks. Beach nets target sharks potentially dangerous to humans and reduce the shark populations to reduce the attacks. The nets' large **(37)** _____ specifically target sharks. Nets also involve "bycatch", which can include killing other **(38)** _____ , like sea turtles, dugongs, dolphins and whales. One way to avoid bycatch is to use drumlines.

Questions 39 and 40

Complete the diagram below of a drumline set-up.

Write NO MORE THAN THREE WORDS from the listening for each answer.

Drumline Set-up

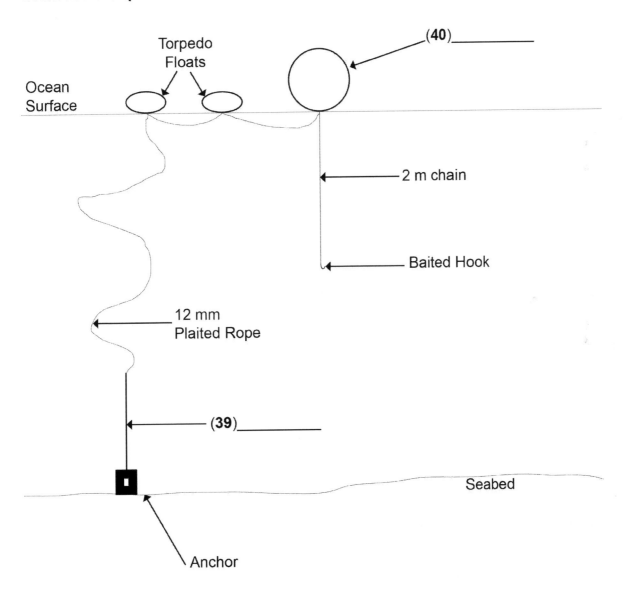

ACADEMIC READING PRACTICE TEST

Reading Passage 1

You should spend about 20 minutes on Questions 1 - 13, based on Reading Passage 1 below.

Biodegradable Plastics

With advances in technology and the increase in global population, plastic materials have found wide applications in every aspect of life and industry. However, most conventional plastics are non-biodegradable, and their increasing accumulation in the environment has become an ecological threat.

Biodegradable plastics are seen by many as a promising solution to this problem, because they are environmentally friendly. Biodegradable plastics offer a lot of advantages, such as increased earth fertility, a low accumulation of bulky plastic materials in the environment (which would certainly minimise injuries to wild animals), a reduction in the cost of waste management and the fact that they can be derived from renewable feedstock, thereby reducing greenhouse gas emissions.

The theory that people like to believe is that biodegradable plastic is synthesised in a factory from plant ingredients and then moulded to create whatever product is required. After the product life is over, decomposition breaks the plastic down to carbon dioxide, which in turn can be returned to plants in nature through photosynthesis. The plant materials can then become part of the plastic creation process again. The key part of this process is the decomposition, which will be looked at in more detail below.

So, what are biodegradable plastics? Biodegradable plastics are plastics that can be broken down by microorganisms such as bacteria or fungi. It is important to note that biodegradable plastics are not necessarily made from biomaterial (i.e. plants). Several biodegradable plastics are even made from oil, in the same way as conventional plastics. It is also important to note the distinction between plastics that are degradable, biodegradable and compostable. People should be cautious when they see a plastic product that advertises that it is 'degradable,' but not 'biodegradable' or "compostable," because this is nothing special. These three terms are not really different 'classes' of plastic, in the sense of being separate sets. They are subsets of one another: all compostable plastics are biodegradable, and all biodegradable plastics are degradable. There are many methods that can be used to break down degradable plastic, but this often just reduces it to extremely small pieces of the same plastic. Over a matter of years, it is possible for the pieces to become small enough to be assimilated by, and be harmful to, wild creatures.

When something is biodegradable, it means it is degradable, but it also means something more: it means that it can be broken down by the metabolism of microorganisms. When a plastic is biodegradable, it can be digested, so that the carbon atoms in the chains of the polymer are broken apart and can actually participate in the creation of other organic molecules. They can be processed by, and become safe parts of, organic living things. This returns them to nature in a very real sense: they become part of the carbon cycle of the ecology of the earth.

When something is compostable, it means that it biodegrades, but it also means that it will degrade within a certain amount of time, under certain conditions. For many types of degradable plastic, it is possible to say that it will break down 'eventually,' but if it were to be sealed in an airtight room, this could take thousands of years.

Using biodegradable plastics as an environmentally friendly solution for things such as plastic bags seems sensible at first glance, but is it really better for the environment? There is a growing environmental lobby that feels that the rubbish issue should be solved by changing people's attitudes rather than by changing the products they are throwing away. Making products biodegradable may actually make the problem of rubbish worse, by making people think that it is acceptable to throw away valuable resources like plastics. For example, a biodegradable plastic bag that's thrown into a hedge will still take years to disappear, rather than days, as some people believe. Even a thrown away banana skin needs one to three years before it is biodegraded. What is more, biodegradable plastics require specific conditions to biodegrade properly, including the presence of micro-organisms, temperature, and humidity, and if not managed properly, they may be worse for the environment than conventional plastics. When biodegradable plastics are put into landfill, which should always be avoided in any case, they produce harmful greenhouse gases when breaking down.

So what are biodegradable plastics good for? In principle, plastics are valued for their ability to make strong, durable products, for example in food storage, transport, building and construction. Biodegradability should therefore be regarded as an additional functionality when the application demands a cheap way to dispose of the item after it has fulfilled its job. One theoretical example of a useful biodegradable product can be found in the food packaging industry. The packaging itself can be composted together with its contents when the product is past its sell-by date or spoiled. There are plenty of other examples such as in agriculture or medicine.

In conclusion, it is a mistake to focus on finding ways to make products easier to throw away in the name of helping the environment. Biodegradable plastics are exciting and useful materials, but they should only be used when they have a definite benefit for a specific product. The best way to help save the planet is to save energy and improve ways of recycling and recovering all plastics.

Questions 1 and 2

Label the diagram below.

Write NO MORE THAN ONE WORD from the text for each answer.

Write your answers in boxes 1 and 2 on your answer sheet.

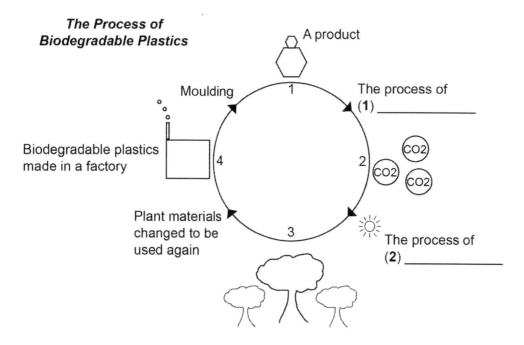

Questions 3 - 7

Choose the correct letter A, B, C or D.

Write the correct letter in boxes 3 - 7 on your answer sheet.

3   One benefit of biodegradable plastics is that

A   wildlife can feed on the end results.
B   they take up less room in landfill.
C   they break down quickly in landfill.
D   they can improve the fertility of the soil.

4   To be classed as a biodegradable plastic, it must

A   originate from plant material.
B   be able to be broken down by microscopic bodies.
C   be disintegrated by carbon dioxide exposure.
D   have some fossil fuel oil in it.

5   If a plastic is compostable,

A   it must also be biodegradable.
B   it cannot also be degradable.
C   it can be broken down to very small plastic pieces.
D   it cannot also be recyclable.

6   Degradable plastics can

A   not be recycled once the degrading process has started.
B   only be broken down with the presence of oxygen.
C   all be safely disposed of in the ground.
D   still be absorbed by some animals.

7   Biodegradable plastics can become

A   a key part of biofuel resources.
B   parts in the bicycle industry.
C   part of the harmless formation of different organic molecules.
D   non-degradable very easily.

Questions 8 – 13

Do the following statements agree with the information given in the text?

In boxes 8 – 13 on your answer sheet write:

TRUE	**if the statement agrees with the information**
FALSE	**if the statement contradicts the information**
NOT GIVEN	**if there is no information on this**

8   Compostable plastics can break down in the required time in any circumstances.

9   If people are not careful, biodegradable plastics could make the waste problem worse.

10   Biodegradable plastics planned for use in the construction industry are currently going through an approval process.

11   Biodegradable plastics can produce unsafe by-products when breaking down.

12   Biodegradable plastic is already being used with food that can be disposed of into the ground together with it.

13   Farming is one industry where biodegradable products can be useful.

Reading Passage 2

You should spend about 20 minutes on Questions 14 - 26, which are based on Reading Passage 2 below.

Australia's Pearling Industry

Paragraph A

Australia's pearling industry began long before European settlement. Northern Australian coastal-dwelling Aborigines harvested the abundant pearl shell from the shallow waters and had a well-established trading network for it. Aborigines also traded with fishermen from the Indonesian island of Sulawesi, who harvested various fish, sea animals and pearl shells. Folklore, songs, cave paintings and the diaries of early settlers tell us of links between Australia and Indonesia dating back 500 years. When Europeans settled in Australia, they were quick to see the value of the pearl fields. Pearling began in earnest in the 1850's at Shark Bay, Western Australia, and this spread to the islands in the Torres Strait over the next 30 years. The colony of Queensland recognised the value of this resource, and annexed the islands in 1879. By 1910, nearly 400 boats and more than 3,500 people were fishing for shell in waters around Broome, then the biggest pearling centre in the world.

Paragraph B

Pearl shell obtained from Western Australia and the Torres Strait found an initial ready market in the clothing industry in the United States and England, especially for buttons and buckles. Quick immediate returns could be made with pearl shell attracting £400 a ton in the early period and, at the worst time, in 1894, £79 a ton. The Torres Strait supplied over half the world demand for pearl shell in the 1890's. Pearl shell and mother of pearl were the main focus of the industry, as the shell was used in developing markets to make cutlery, hair combs, jewellery items, as well as art objects and inlay for furniture. One business alone in the Torres Strait raised £31,500 worth of shell and £5000 worth of pearls in one year.

Paragraph C

These boom times attracted large numbers of Europeans, South Sea Islanders and Asians who came for the adventure, the promise of work and the possibility of making their fortunes. In the Torres Strait, by 1886, there were an equal number of non-islanders as there were islanders. In Broome, the largest of these immigrant groups were the Chinese. Not only did they come as pearlers, but also as cooks and shopkeepers, similar to the gold boom days.

Paragraph D

In the Torres Strait, pearlers not only sought pearls, but also other island resources to maintain the industry and this extended to the ransacking of the islands for food and timber and water to eat and build with. Along with the onslaught of diseases, this contributed to a significant population decline amongst the Torres Strait islanders within 30 years to as low as 50 per cent of pre-pearling populations by 1900.

Paragraph E

From 1862, the pearl supply was so low that larger boats were sent out two kilometres off shore to collect oysters in deep water. Aboriginal men and women would 'naked dive'.
This meant they had to dive down deep with no oxygen, no snorkel and no mask. In the Torres Strait, employment conditions were regarded as dangerous as well as unspeakably squalid and this contributed to many accidents. Many of the Japanese divers were used as indentured labour. This means that they were working for no money in order to repay a debt, usually for their transportation to Australia. Divers were paid by the amount of shell they collected and very few of these divers ever managed to work off their debt. Attempts to regulate the marine industry and to prevent improper employment of Aborigines and islanders were made by the Queensland parliament and wages were required to be paid in front of an inspector after 1893.

Paragraph F

The invention of diving suits revolutionised the pearling industry in Australia. Divers could go deeper than ever before, stay underwater longer and collect more shell and pearls. These divers wore vulcanised canvas suits and massive bronze helmets and spent hours underwater. On the bottom, they struggled about in lead-weighted boots, frantically scooping oysters into bags, because divers were paid by the amount of shell they collected. Pearl divers regularly faced the threat of shark attack, as well as the dreaded crippling effects of the bends with every dive. Some sources say that the mortality rate for divers was 50 per cent. In addition, whole fleets were shipwrecked in single cyclones.

Paragraph G

During World War 1 and World War 2, the industry virtually ceased, as most of the workers enlisted. The industry relied heavily on its Japanese pearl divers and as a result of Japan entering World War 2, these divers were detained in prisoner of war camps. The recovery after World War 2 was slow, as harvesting methods used in the previous decades meant that the supply of shell had almost run out. The development of cultured pearls and the use of plastic buttons and buckles in the 1950's also devastated the industry in the Torres Strait by the 1960's.

Paragraph H

Broome and the pearling industry survived the economic devastation of both World Wars and today is recognised as a 'pearl capital.' Today, Western Australia has a well-established industry including hatchery and culturing facilities, producing pearls valued at AUS$150 million last year. As a result of the pearling industry, the architecture and population of Broome is quite unique in Australia. It has a Chinatown with a number of Chinese buildings and a local cemetery with both Japanese and Chinese sections. Broome's location in the sub-tropics has contributed to its attraction as a tourist destination with a thriving multicultural community and flourishing economy.

Glossary

Cultured pearl – An artificially created pearl, done by inserting a small plastic ball into the oyster.

Questions 14 – 21

The text on the previous pages has 8 paragraphs (A – H).

Choose the correct heading for each paragraph from the list of headings below.

Write the correct number (i – xi) in boxes 14 – 21 on your answer sheet.

i	The Industry's Negative Local Effects
ii	Local Governments Benefit through Taxation
iii	Developments and Dangers
iv	High Demand Brings Large Profits
v	Boats Designed for the Industry
vi	Industry Setbacks
vii	The Origins of the Industry
viii	Shameful Exploitation
ix	The Legacy
x	The Rush for Riches
xi	Government Legislation Affects Pricing

14   Paragraph A

15   Paragraph B

16   Paragraph C

17   Paragraph D

18   Paragraph E

19   Paragraph F

20   Paragraph G

21   Paragraph H

Questions 22 - 26

Answer the questions below.

Write NO MORE THAN THREE WORDS from the text for each answer.

Write your answers in boxes 22 - 26 on your answer sheet.

22   To which industry was Australian pearl shell first sold?

23   What construction resource was over-exploited on the Torres Strait islands to help support the pearl industry there?

24   Who supervised any money paid to Aboriginal and island workers from 1893?

25   What hindered pearlers in diving suits from walking properly on the sea bed?

26   What had depleted the available amount of pearl shell before World War 2?

Reading Passage 3

You should spend about 20 minutes on Questions 27 - 40, which are based on Reading Passage 3 below.

Blood Type Dieting

A link between ABO blood groups and diet was proposed by Dr. Peter. J. D'Adamo in his book "Eat Right For Your Type," published a few years ago. Dr. D'Adamo claims that the ABO blood groups reveal the dietary habits of our ancestors and adherence to a diet specific to one's blood group can improve health and decrease risk of chronic conditions, such as cardiovascular disease. D'Adamo's theory is based on the idea that each blood group has its own unique antigen marker and this marker reacts badly with certain foods, leading to all sorts of potential health problems and harmful weight gain. Furthermore, Dr. D'Adamo believes that levels of stomach acidity and digestive enzymes are linked with people's blood types. Consequently, he says, by following a diet designed specifically for someone's blood type, the body digests and absorbs food more efficiently, with the result that the subject loses weight.

The theory is based on how humans developed during their existence. Dr. D'Adamo believes that because blood types evolved at different times throughout history, we should eat a diet based on the types of foods our ancestors typically ate at the time when our blood type first emerged. As humans migrated and were forced to adapt their diets to local conditions, the new diets provoked changes in their digestive tracts and immune systems, necessary for them to first survive and later thrive in their new habitats. Different foods metabolised in a unique manner by each individual with a different ABO blood group probably resulted in that blood group achieving a certain level of susceptibility to the endemic bacteria, viruses and parasites of the area. This probably more than any other factor was what has influenced the modern day distribution of blood groups.

Based on the blood type diet theory, group O is considered the ancestral blood group in humans and was the first to emerge. This is difficult to prove, but there are communities today that can provide evidence for this conclusion. There is an extraordinarily high percentage of blood group O people in isolated populations, as well as it being the most common in the world at large. Even though early migrations dispersed the gene for group O blood throughout the world, because of their geographic locations these unique societies have remained isolated from interaction with other populations. If A, B and O had developed simultaneously, the isolated population groups would have had all of them. But these 'old societies' are group O, because genes for the later blood groups never had the opportunity to enter into their populations. They have remained unchanged. From a purely scientific point of view, chemical analysis of the group O antigen also reveals that, from a structural perspective, it is the simplest blood group and it serves as the backbone for the synthesis of the increasingly complex A, B and AB. As a result, Dr. D'Adamo advises that the optimal diet for people with group O blood should resemble the high animal protein diets typical of the hunter-gatherer era, which matches this oldest of blood groups.

Next came the emergence of blood type A, sometime around 15,000 B.C. By this time, the human ancestors had settled down into an agrarian culture. The creation of blood type A around this time meant our ancestors did well on a vegetarian-based diet and so Dr. D'Adamo recommends that blood group A's should today follow a similar diet.

Blood type B supposedly evolved around 10,000 B.C thanks to humanity's nomadic ancestors. They abandoned their farms and started wandering the land, constantly moving from place to place. Consequently, Dr. D'Adamo's theory holds that blood group B's today can get away with eating a varied diet that consists of most foods including meat, dairy, grains and vegetables.

Finally came blood type AB, which evolved just 1,000 years ago. Dr. D'Adamo thinks this blood type helped our ancestors make the transition to contemporary times. This means that people with blood group AB can eat a mixture of the foods suitable for both blood group A and blood group B.

Medical experts universally agree that the theory is nonsense, and say there is absolutely no link between our blood group and the diet we eat. Consequently, you will not find qualified nutritionists or dietitians recommending this diet. There are also several concerns from nutritionists, namely that the diets recommended for blood groups O and A are considerably limited and cut out major groups of foods. In the long term, this can result in a poor intake of nutrients needed for good health. Cutting out dairy products, for example, will lead to poor intakes of calcium, which can put people at risk of osteoporosis, while avoiding meat can result in low intakes of iron, which can lead to anaemia.

In spite of all this, blood type diets captivate people and have faithful adherents who swear to their efficacy. It is perhaps the anthropologic significance of the theory that fascinates. There is something very intellectually and emotionally riveting about understanding the ebb and flow of human experience and linking it to people's health today. Not only is it therefore fascinating from an intellectual standpoint, but people also can see, feel and touch the modern day physical ramifications of these long ago events.

Glossary

antigen marker - a substance that the body uses to recognise alien attacks.

osteoporosis – a disease making bones brittle and easy to break.

anaemia – a lack of red blood cells or haemoglobin in the blood.

© US Government - ncbi.nlm.nih.gov

Questions 27 – 29

Complete each sentence with the correct ending (A - F) below.

Write the correct letter (A - F) in answer boxes 27 - 29 on your answer sheet.

27   D'Adamo claims that following a blood group diet can

28   D'Adamo claims that eating the wrong food can

29   Migration around the world to areas with different conditions can

A   explain why different blood groups evolved in different locations.

B   be done in groups at particular diet centres.

C   cause adverse bodily reactions leading to weight gain.

D   lead to incurable diseases.

E   improve the health of the dieter's heart.

F   be the reason for certain facial characteristics.

Questions 30 – 35

Complete the table below.

Write NO MORE THAN TWO WORDS from the text for each answer.

Write your answers in boxes 30 - 35 on your answer sheet.

Diets According to Blood Groups		
Blood Group	**Background**	**Diet Required**
O	* The first, the most **(30)** _____ and the simplest * The **(31)** _____ for the other blood groups	* Rich in animal protein due to **(32)** _____ background of this time.
A	* Humanity became an **(33)** _____ society.	* Nutrition vegetarian-based.
B	* Part of humanity became **(34)** _____ and left their farm life.	* A varied diet.
AB	* The most recent * AB facilitated the **(35)** _____ to modern life	* A mixture of A and B foods

Questions 36 – 40

Do the following statements agree with the views of the writer of the text?

In boxes 36 - 40 on your answer sheet write:

YES	**if the statement agrees with the writer's views**
NO	**if the statement doesn't agree with the writer's views**
NOT GIVEN	**if it is impossible to say what the writer thinks about this**

36   It is unlikely that people will be advised by a health professional to follow a blood group diet.

37   Supporters of the blood group diet assert the diet should be followed in conjunction with supplements.

38   A lack of dairy products in a diet can put people at risk of having too few red blood cells.

39   The idea of a relationship of the blood group diet with human evolution is responsible for people's preoccupation with it.

40   The blood group migration theories have helped scientists to explain the incidence of various diseases throughout history.

ACADEMIC WRITING PRACTICE TEST

TASK 1

You should spend about 20 minutes on this task.

The table below shows statistics relating to students on UK and England only higher education courses for two periods of time.

Summarise the information by selecting and reporting the main features, and make comparisons where relevant.

You should write at least 150 words.

All Students on UK and England only Higher Education Courses for 2003 - 2004 and 2013 - 2014

	Undergraduate Full-time	Undergraduate Part-time	Postgraduate Full-time	Postgraduate Part-time	Total Higher Education
ALL UK (England, Wales, Scotland & Northern Ireland) HIGHER EDUCATION INSTITUTIONS					
2003 - 2004	997,661	394,946	140,909	222,663	1,756,179
2013 - 2014	1,232,005	572,965	248,380	252,755	2,306,105
% increase	23%	45%	76%	14%	31%
ALL ENGLAND ONLY HIGHER EDUCATION INSTITUTIONS					
2003 - 2004	807,138	352,459	115,729	183,358	1,458,684
2013 - 2014	1,011,955	493,060	206,865	210,300	1,922,180
% increase	25%	40%	79%	15%	32%

TASK 2

You should spend about 40 minutes on this task.

Write about the following topic:

The pressures of today's society often mean that both parents in a family have to work and this creates a poor environment for children to grow up in. Discuss this situation and give your opinion.

You should write at least 250 words.

ACADEMIC SPEAKING PRACTICE TEST

Section 1

- Can you describe the city/town/village where you live?
- Is this a good place to live?
- Would you prefer to live in a city or in the countryside? (Why?)

Topic 1   Smoking

- Do you smoke? (Why/Why not?)
- At what age do you think smoking should be legal?
- Do you think that smoking should be banned from all indoor places, as has already happened in some countries?
- How can governments stop people from smoking?

Topic 2   Social Media

- Why do you think social media is so popular nowadays?
- How do you think social media will change over the next 10 years?
- What are some of the dangers that social media can represent?
- How can we reduce the fascination that young people have with social media, or shouldn't we be worried?

Section 2

> Describe a memorable journey that you once took
>   You should say:
>   where this journey was
>   when this journey was
>   what you did during the journey
> and explain why this journey is so memorable for you.

Section 3

Topic 1   Travel

- Why do you think people enjoy travel?
- What can people learn from travel?
- How has travel changed over the last 50 years?
- What are some of the negative impacts of so much travel nowadays?

Topic 2   Air Travel

- What are some of the dangers of air travel?
- What are some of the reasons that budget air travel has increased so much in popularity recently?
- How do you feel air travel will change over the next 30 years?
- Should governments restrict the amount of air travel nowadays and how could they do this?

ACADEMIC PRACTICE TEST ANSWERS

LISTENING TEST ANSWERS				READING TEST ANSWERS			
1	Carol	21	seminars	1	Decomposition	21	ix
2	34	22	accents	2	Photosynthesis	22	(The) clothing (industry)
3	HT8 5RD	23	children	3	D	23	Timber
4	Credit card	24	names	4	B	24	An inspector
5	Economy (size)	25	marketing	5	A	25	Lead(-weighted) (boots)
6	(An) emergency pack	26	(language) variation	6	D	26	Harvesting (methods)
7	45 litres	27	supervisor	7	C	27	E
8	(At) (the) airport	28	deadlines	8	FALSE	28	C
9	(A) (basic) map	29	survey	9	TRUE	29	A
10	(About) a mile	30	statistics	10	NOT GIVEN	30	common
11	4	31	freshwater	11	TRUE	31	backbone
12	(management) committee	32	critical list	12	TRUE	32	hunter-gatherer
13	volunteers	33	(fierce) appearance	13	TRUE	33	agrarian
14	(local) government (area)	34	identification	14	vii	34	nomadic
15	staff	35	breeding cycle	15	iv	35	transition
16	matches	36	habitat	16	x	36	YES
17	musicians	37	hole size	17	i	37	NOT GIVEN
18	dance	38	(endangered) species	18	viii	38	NO
19	(local) police	39	(Heavy) chain	19	iii	39	YES
20	maps	40	(A) (marker) float	20	vi	40	NOT GIVEN

/ indicates an alternative answer
( ) indicates an optional part of answer

Note: The Listening Test transcript showing answers' locations in sentences can be downloaded on our website: visit http://www.ielts-blog.com/book-practice-test/

WRITING TEST MODEL RESPONSES

TASK 1

This report is about a table giving statistics on students on Higher Education Courses in the UK and only in England, comparing the years 2003 to 2004 with the years 2013 to 2014. The table summarises the statistics into percentage increases, to make it clearer how much student numbers in higher education courses have increased.

In institutions in all of the UK, the sector that had the largest growth in students was the Postgraduate full-time course with a 76% increase from 2003 to 2014. Even though this course saw the greatest improvement, the higher education course with the most students in both periods was the Undergraduate full-time course with 997,661 students in 2003 to 2004 and 1,232,005 students in 2013 to 2014.

In institutions in only England, the Postgraduate full-time course was also the one to experience the most growth with an increase of 79% from 2003 to 2014. The other courses had percentage increases ranging from 15 to 40 per cent. Again, the higher education course with the most students in both periods was the Undergraduate full-time course with 807,138 students in 2003 to 2004 and 1,011,955 students in 2013 to 2014.

In conclusion, it is clear that the number of students increased significantly for the time periods in all courses in both the UK and only in England.

TASK 2

Nowadays, in spite of having children, many women work in addition to their husbands. The question of who is to care for the children if both parents are employed is a sensitive one, as, when both parents are working, children are raised in a poorer environment.

When looking around today, more childcare facilities offer whole day care, so that parents can pick up their children after work. The children therefore do not experience the same love for these hours as they would if their mother took care of them. As children get older, the situation can worsen. Many primary and especially secondary schools end early in the day. Children are therefore unsupervised for long hours. This can lead to children making bad choices or to loneliness. Therefore, it is clear the development of children can be negatively impacted when both parents are working.

However, the issue is not this simple, as provisions have been made to decrease the negative effects. In many countries, there are not only day care facilities available, but also all-day schools have been created to ensure that children are taken care of when their parents are working. Furthermore, these facilities also lead to children being in stronger contact with children of the same age, which can benefit their development.

In conclusion, while negative impacts on development can be seen, if appropriate measures are taken, a child's development can be impacted positively through other means, such as ensuring the time families can spend together is used well.

SPEAKING SAMPLE PRACTICE TEST – Examiner's Commentary

Please download the Speaking Sample Practice test recording and transcript on the following web page: http://www.ielts-blog.com/book-practice-test/

Below is the Examiner's Commentary on Katrin's performance in the recorded Speaking test, including her estimated IELTS Band Score.

Examiner's Commentary

The person interviewed is Katrin, a German female. Katrin is an office administrator.

Section 1

Katrin spoke fluently and accurately. She did not need to pause for language and gave full answers. She had a good vocabulary range, though she used the occasional awkward choice ("metropole" and "to their side" instead of 'at their sides'). There were very few grammar errors. Katrin had an accent, but a it was often negligible.

Section 2

Katrin spoke fluently for the allocated time. Her pronunciation was again very good, though she showed an error with pronouncing the 'v' in ("visited" and "individual"), which is not uncommon for Germans. There were a few minor grammar and word choice errors ("the first time I did that" instead of 'I had done that' + "everyone had its own character" instead of 'their own character' + 'did a journey' instead of 'made a journey'). None of the errors created any problems with comprehension.

Section 3

Again, Katrin showed her good ability at English. Her vocabulary choices were good, her grammar mostly accurate and her pronunciation clear. Pauses were only to consider her replies. She showed a sense of humour, which is always a nice thing to do, as it creates a relaxed atmosphere, where people can perform more effectively.

Marking - The marking of the IELTS Speaking Test is done in 4 parts.

Fluency and Coherence	7
Lexical Resource	7
Grammatical Range and Accuracy	7
Pronunciation	8
Estimated IELTS Speaking Band	**7**

Printed in Great Britain
by Amazon.co.uk, Ltd.,
Marston Gate.